Modern and Contemporary Art

The Lannan Collection *at The Art Institute of Chicago*

THE ART INSTITUTE OF CHICAGO *Museum Studies*

THE ART INSTITUTE OF CHICAGO *Museum Studies*
VOLUME 25, NO. 1

© 1999 by The Art Institute of Chicago
ISSN 0069-3235
ISBN 0-86559-174-1

Published semiannually by The Art Institute of Chicago, 111 South Michigan Avenue, Chicago, Illinois
60603-6110. Regular subscription rates: $20 for members of the Art Institute, $25 for other individuals, and
$32 for institutions. Subscribers outside the U.S.A. should add $10 per year for postage. For more information, call (312) 443-3540 or consult our Web site at www.artic.edu/aic/books.

For individuals, single copies are $15 each. For institutions, all single copies are $19 each. For orders of
single copies outside the U.S.A., please add $5 per copy. Back issues are available from The Art Institute of
Chicago Museum Shop or from the Publications Department of the Art Institute at the address above.

Editor: Britt Salvesen, with Margherita Andreotti, Gregory Nosan, and Susan F. Rossen; Photo Editors:
Sarah Gordon and Stacey Hendricks; Designer: Ann M. Wassmann; Production: Sarah E. Guernsey;
Subscription and Circulation Manager: Bryan D. Miller.

Unless otherwise noted, all works in the Art Institute's collections were photographed by the Department of
Imaging, Alan Newman, Executive Director. Permission to reproduce the works of art in this volume has
been provided by the artists or their representatives; for credits applying to all images for which separate
acknowledgment is due, see p. 104.

Volume 25, no. 1, was typeset in Stempel Garamond and Officina Sans by Z...Art & Graphics, Chicago;
color separations were made by Professional Graphics, Inc., Rockford, Illinois. The issue was printed by
Litho Inc., St. Paul, Minnesota, and bound by Midwest Editions, Minneapolis, Minnesota.

Front cover: Bruce Nauman (American; born 1941), *Clown Torture* (detail; video still), 1987 (see p. 63).
Back cover: Mike Kelley (American; born 1954), *Eviscerated Corpse*, 1989 (see p. 67).

Ongoing support for *Museum Studies* has been provided by a grant for scholarly catalogues and publications from The Andrew W. Mellon Foundation.

Table of Contents

THE ART INSTITUTE OF CHICAGO

Museum Studies, Volume 25, No. 1
Modern and Contemporary Art: The Lannan Collection
at The Art Institute of Chicago

Jeremy Strick, Guest Editor

Acknowledgments

This issue of *The Art Institute of Chicago Museum Studies*, "Modern and Contemporary Art: The Lannan Collection at The Art Institute of Chicago," has been organized to celebrate the addition of over one hundred works to the museum's collections. It will also serve as a record of these works' distinguished provenance as, with time, they become integrated into the Art Institute's existing and future holdings.

The opportunity to choose gifts and purchases from Lannan Foundation's world-renowned collection of modern and contemporary art was a thrilling one. Representatives of the foundation were unfailingly helpful and generous in facilitating the selection process, which proved to be a collaborative effort between the curators in the Department of Twentieth-Century Painting and Sculpture—Madeleine Grynsztein, former Associate Curator of Contemporary Art, was particularly instrumental—and curators in the Departments of American Arts, Photography, Prints and Drawings, and Textiles.

A similar cooperative spirit has shaped this publication. Overall coordination of the issue was undertaken by the Department of Twentieth-Century Painting and Sculpture. Special thanks are due to Stephanie Skestos, curatorial assistant, who not only contributed entries but also compiled the detailed checklist, assisted fellow authors with research, and acted as liaison with other museum departments. Her efficiency and attention to detail are to be commended.

A team of nine authors wrote entries on thirty-five works in the Lannan collection. These works were selected to display the depth and breadth of the acquisition: its range from the immediate post-war period to the present, its wide variety of media, and its international roster of artists. I thank each of the authors—Andrea D. Barnwell, Stephanie D'Alessandro, Raymond Hernández-Durán, Mark Pascale, James E. Rondeau, Daniel Schulman, Stephanie Skestos, and Colin Westerbeck—for their fine work. Doug Severson of the Department of Photography and Raymond Hernández-Durán of the Department of Prints and Drawings assisted with the media descriptions for works in their areas of expertise.

For photography we are grateful to Lannan Foundation and also to the Art Institute's Department of Imaging, especially Alan Newman, Executive Director, as well as Bill Foster, Christopher Gallagher, Robert Hashimoto, Robert Lifson, Josh Mosley, Brad Nugent, Sydney Orr, Gregory Williams, and Iris Wong. Art handlers Nick Barron and John Tweedie provided capable assistance. The issue's layout is the work of the Art Institute's designer Ann M. Wassmann; Toby Zallman, of Z...Art & Graphics, Chicago, typeset the issue; and ProGraphics, Inc., produced the color separations. Production was in the able hands of Sarah E. Guernsey, assisted by Stacey Hendricks, both of the Publications Department. The work of the editorial team was coordinated by Britt Salvesen; she was assisted by the following colleagues in the Publications Department: Margherita Andreotti, Gregory Nosan, and Susan F. Rossen. Former *Museum Studies* editor Michael Sittenfeld was involved in the early stages of the project; circulation is managed by Bryan D. Miller.

Kathleen Merrill and Jenée Misraje of Lannan Foundation provided invaluable information and assistance at various stages of this project. J. Patrick Lannan, Jr., offered generously of his time and knowledge; we extend our greatest thanks to him and his sisters Patricia Lawler and Sharon Lannan Ferrill, and their colleagues on the Lannan board for their extraordinary and truly historic generosity to The Art Institute of Chicago.

Jeremy Strick

Fixed and Visible: Lannan Foundation and The Art Institute of Chicago

Jeremy Strick

FORMER FRANCES AND THOMAS DITTMER
CURATOR OF TWENTIETH-CENTURY PAINTING AND SCULPTURE

n February 1997, The Art Institute of Chicago announced one of the largest and most important acquisitions in its 118-year history: 106 works from Lannan Foundation came to the museum through a combination of gift and purchase. The works range in date from 1944 to 1995, and in medium from painting and sculpture to printmaking, drawing, photography, and video installation. Prior to the Lannan acquisition, the Art Institute had significant holdings from this period. Following the acquisition, contemporary art became one of the museum's signal strengths.

Along with the Art Institute, two other institutions also announced major gifts from Lannan Foundation: the Museum of Contemporary Art, Los Angeles, received 114 works, and the Museum of Contemporary Art, Chicago, received 85. Subsequently, the foundation has distributed a total of 593 works to 29 public institutions in the United States. The disbursement of Lannan Foundation's collection to museums around the country concluded a remarkable episode in the history of American collecting; it also marked an exceptional moment in the history of American philanthropy.

It is fair to state that, of the many institutions to benefit from Lannan Foundation's largesse, none received a more important group of works than the Art Institute. The Lannan acquisition accomplished three distinct ends for the museum: it augmented existing areas of strength; it created new areas of strength; and it moved the collection in new directions, enhancing our ability to engage with younger generations of artists and viewers.

Clyfford Still's *Untitled* of 1958 (p. 21) is a striking example of a Lannan work that enhances an already outstanding aspect of the Art Institute's collection: its survey of American Abstract Expressionism, which features major works by de Kooning, Pollock, Kline, and Rothko, among others. Still was represented by one of his most exceptional paintings, *1951–52* (1951–52), a vast canvas with a thick, heavily impastoed, black surface, interrupted only at its lower left edge by a thin strip of red. An audacious exploration of the monochrome, it is among the most radical of Still's major works. Lannan Foundation's 1958 canvas offers an ideal complement. Larger, more complex, and with a wider range of colors than its predecessor, the painting exemplifies the kind of heroic, craggy composition that inspired critics to compare Still's work to that of such nineteenth-century American landscapists as Frederic Edwin Church. These two canvases represent the essential range and ambition of Still's mature oeuvre at a level of quality exceeded by no other public collection.

Other pieces allowed the Art Institute to establish entirely new areas of concentration. For example the museum owned two works by the German artist Gerhard Richter when the opportunity arose to acquire all twenty-two of Lannan Foundation's Richters—ten paintings on canvas, three paintings on color photographs, and a set of nine lithographs. Richter is now represented at the Art Institute by a group of works spanning a thirty-year period, from one of his earliest surviving paintings, *Mouth* of 1963 (p. 25), to a rare floral still life, *Flowers* of 1993 (p. 19). The museum has become one of the world's great repositories for the art of this exceptionally influential figure, and boasts the most comprehensive selection of his work of any American institution. Many of these paintings are currently installed in a single gallery devoted to Richter's work, a new highlight of the museum's twentieth-century collection.

Finally, the Lannan acquisition assures that, for another generation at least, the Art Institute's global, historical survey of the highlights of human aesthetic production will include certain of our most compelling recent achievements. A number of works by younger artists who were introduced to the collection through the Lannan acquisition now enliven the museum's contemporary galleries. Mike Kelley's *Eviscerated Corpse* of 1989 (p. 67), Alfredo Jaar's *1+1+1* of 1987 (p. 59), three large photographs by Thomas Ruff of 1986 and 1988 (p. 55–57), and Felix Gonzalez-Torres's *Untitled (Last Light)* of 1993 (p. 85), to name just a few examples, add new currency and suggest future directions to the Art Institute's contemporary program.

Works from Lannan Foundation allow the Art Institute to describe the development of twentieth-century art in a far more comprehensive and detailed fashion than was previously possible. The earliest object acquired, Robert Motherwell's 1944 *Wall Painting with Stripes* (p. 13), adds to our holdings of early New York School Abstract Expressionism. Sam Francis's *In Lovely Blueness* (p. 17) and Jay De Feo's *The Annunciation* (p. 19), both painted in the mid-1950s, suggest some of the ways in which a subsequent generation of artists, many working at a distance from New York, adapted the means and meanings of Abstract Expressionism. Elements of Pop Art and Minimalism are wittily melded in Richard Artschwager's *Table with Pink Tablecloth* of 1964 (p. 27), while Brice Marden's *Rodeo* of 1971 (p. 45), with its clear, geometric structure and enigmatic surface, presents elements associated with Postminimalism. Richter, whose work emerged out of Pop Art in the early 1960s, has since addressed the contradictory natures of both representation and abstraction, as well as the interplay between painting and photography. This last relationship is also explored by Chuck Close, whose painting, Polaroids, and prints of fellow artist Alex Katz (pp. 87–88) in the collection exemplify contemporary portraiture at its most compelling and, preserved as a group, reveal Close's working methods. Bruce Nauman is another prominent figure represented in the Lannan acquisition by works in several media, most significantly his 1987 installation *Clown Torture* (p. 63), a powerful, humorous, and disturbing piece with many of the qualities that have made video projection a defining medium of the 1990s. Photographic works by artists such as Ruff and Lucas Samaras (see p. 49) demonstrate the increasingly central role of photography in contemporary art, and the consistent erosion of media hierarchies that has been a hallmark of our time.

Even while works from Lannan Foundation add to the Art Institute's presentation of contemporary art, those same works are linked by another history: that of the foundation itself. From its origins as a personal collection to its growth as a foundation that decisively influenced the contemporary art world; from its ultimate dispersal of the collection to its current role as a leading grantmaker in various areas of cultural activity—Lannan Foundation has traversed a remarkable history. That history is now inscribed, as it were, on the walls of the Art Institute, whose collection includes objects acquired by J. Patrick Lannan, Sr., and by the foundation directed by his children. Two generations of taste are represented in our galleries, as are changing ideas about the nature and purposes of art.

The history of Lannan Foundation is, in important respects, a Chicago story. J. Patrick Lannan, Sr., found his passion for culture in this city, and his tastes in art were shaped at the Art Institute. Through gifts to the Art Institute and to the Museum of Contemporary Art, Chicago, the foundation maintains a prominent role in the city's cultural life. One could say that, with the 1997 announcement of its gifts to Chicago institutions, an important part of Lannan Foundation's collection came home.

Lannan Foundation was established in 1960 by J. Patrick Lannan, Sr., an entrepreneur and financier with a passion for literature (especially poetry) and avant-garde art. Born in Sterling, Illinois, in 1905, the eldest son of an Irish cabinetmaker, in his late teens Joseph Patrick Lannan trained as an electrician for the Ford Motor Company in Michigan; he entered the business world a few years later after moving to Chicago, where he found a job as a bond salesman. When his employer went bankrupt at the onset of the Depression, Lannan switched to buying defaulted bonds for another Chicago firm, Kneeland & Co. By 1932 he was able to buy a one-third interest in the company.

After World War II, Lannan embarked on a career of buying and reorganizing poorly performing businesses. He first acquired Federal Electric Co., which manufactured sirens and signals, and then bought Henry Holt & Co., a publishing firm. Lannan soon established a pattern of quickly and secretly moving in to take over troubled companies, and swiftly and decisively reorganizing them. Often his strategy involved shedding money-losing divisions in order better to concentrate upon a firm's core profitable business. Lannan objected to being labeled a corporate raider, noting that he almost always retained stock and a board position in the companies he purchased and transformed. His success derived not from quick turnovers, but rather from the substantial and sustained increases in profitability resulting from his initial decisions.

Although he was known as an extremely tough businessman with a firm dollars-and-cents view of any transaction, Lannan had a lifelong dedication to liberal political and social causes. As a young man, he was fired from his first electrician's job with the Ford Motor Company for expressing "bolshevist" sentiments. Later in his life, as he achieved financial prosperity, he actively supported such organizations as the National Association for the Advancement of Colored People (NAACP) and the American Civil Liberties Union (ACLU), and worked for the presidential campaign of Robert Kennedy. Lannan's social concerns motivated certain activities of the foundation that he eventually established, and continue to do so today.

The beginnings of Lannan's interest in art and culture can be traced to the early 1950s. Then living in Chicago's Hyde Park neighborhood, he formed a friendship with a neighbor, the attorney and judge Augustin Bowes. Bowes, who had long been involved with *Poetry* magazine, an independent monthly published in Chicago, encouraged Lannan to read avant-garde literature and verse, thus engaging him in the process that opened his mind to art and culture. Lannan started to visit the Art Institute, and began his collection with purchases from the art gallery in Marshall Field's department store.

An important resource for Lannan in these early years was Katharine Kuh. Named the Art Institute's first Curator of Modern Painting and Sculpture in 1954 (the museum's autonomous Department of Twentieth-Century Painting and Sculpture was established in the late 1960s), Kuh exerted enormous influence over Chicago's cultural life in the years before and after World War II. Under her tutelage, Lannan's interest in and knowledge of modern art grew considerably, as did his sophistication. One important work that Kuh advised him to buy was Alberto Giacometti's *Tall Figure* of 1947, which Lannan donated to the Art Institute in 1959 (see fig. 2).

By the mid-1950s, art and culture had become the central focus of Lannan's life. A typical day might find him being driven to an artist's studio, reading a novel or a book of poetry on the way, and planning to attend the theater that night. His reactions to works of art were swift, direct, and even passionate; although he acquired significant historical knowledge, he retained trust in his visceral responses. Above all, Lannan loved to enter into and experience the creative process. He liked nothing better than to visit artists' studios and to converse with artists and writers (see fig. 1). An aggressive businessman, he was a tough

FIGURE 1 Joseph Patrick Lannan, Sr., with Isamu Noguchi, 1971. Photo: courtesy Lannan Foundation.

negotiator on prices, but was always mindful of his role in helping those artists whose work he admired.

At this time, Lannan's collection included drawings by Delacroix and Picasso, sculpture by Giacometti, and Abstract Expressionist paintings by Joan Mitchell (whose mother, Marion Strobel, had been an editor of *Poetry*). As the 1950s progressed, Lannan became increasingly committed to Abstract Expressionism. By 1959 he had acquired paintings by James Brooks, Motherwell, Theodore Stamos, and Still, as well as sculpture by Isamu Noguchi. He also sought out artists who were just beginning to establish their reputations. Lannan viewed his collecting strategies and business methods as mirroring one another. In both areas, he looked for what he described as "special situations": undervalued companies and underrecognized artists whose work would come to be appreciated. "What fun is it to buy a Picasso?" Lannan once rhetorically asked a writer for *Forbes* magazine. "It's the same as buying stock in General Motors."

Even though Lannan drew connections between his art buying and his business practices, and enjoyed seeing his acquisitions rise in value, he did not view his collecting as a profit-making enterprise. A self-made man, he did not believe in inherited wealth, and he was determined to arrange for the meaningful disposition of his art collection and his considerable estate. In 1960, therefore, he established the foundation that would manage his collection and administer his charitable activities. Perhaps surprisingly, however, Lannan Foundation then had very few strictures and little definition; it was set up as an Illinois not-for-profit foundation, to be run by a board of directors who were mostly members of Lannan's family, as is still the case today.

Lannan owned residences in three cities: Chicago, New York, and Palm Beach, Florida. Paintings and sculpture were displayed in all three homes, but the bulk of the foundation's holdings found their way to the Palm Beach house, where Lannan installed his collection salon-style, hanging paintings one above the other. In order to maintain the foundation's tax-exempt status, the collection had to be accessible to the public, an issue Lannan resolved by allowing regular tours of the house.

In 1979 Lannan became aware that the city of Palm Beach intended to invoke zoning restrictions to forbid the tours of his house. In response he decided to establish a separate, public gallery for the collection. After locating an art deco movie theater in the neighboring town of Lake Worth, he employed the architect Mark Hampton to renovate and redesign it. The Lannan Museum opened its doors in 1981.

The collection displayed in Lake Worth was remarkably eclectic. In addition to the Abstract Expressionist paintings acquired in the 1950s, it included a significant representation of color-field painting, with important canvases by such artists as Morris Louis and Kenneth Noland, as well as Minimalist works by Donald Judd and Frank Stella, and sculpture by Mark di Suvero. Pop Art, to which Lannan never responded, was absent from the installation, but a notable presence was his collection of crafts: over one thousand glass and ceramic objects, textiles, and kinetic sculpture. In 1974, discouraged by the rising prices of contemporary paintings, Lannan had found in crafts a new "special situation," and he was active in this field until 1980, his enthusiasm finding parallels in the mixed-media work of artists such as John Ahearn (see p. 53), Keith Haring (see p. 90), and Kelley (see p. 67).

Fighting emphysema in his last years, Lannan nonetheless maintained a remarkable level of energy and activity, and continued to pursue his strong interest in art and culture. Indeed, on the last day of his life, in 1983, he visited the Marian Goodman Gallery, New York. His accomplishments in business and art patronage were matched by his support for literature. He served for over thirty years as Chairman of the Board of the Modern Poetry Association,

and he helped to create Poetry Day, *Poetry* magazine's annual fundraising event, when he brought Robert Frost to Chicago to read in 1956. Poetry Day continues as the magazine's annual benefit and anniversary celebration.

Following Lannan's death, it took nearly three years to settle his estate. Finally in 1986 Lannan's children found themselves largely responsible for a foundation that had been bequeathed assets of eighty million dollars, but had no clear direction. By family consent, leadership of the foundation fell to Lannan's youngest son, J. Patrick Lannan, Jr. When their father's interest in the arts began to blossom, J. Patrick Lannan, Jr., an adolescent, was still living at home and in the company of his father visited museums, galleries, and studios, and conversed with writers, artists, and critics. The family turned to him as the person who could best guide them through the world their father had inhabited. Although the two men were temperamental opposites— Lannan, Jr., is as soft-spoken and contemplative as Lannan, Sr., was reactive and expressive—the son shares his father's passionate dedication to art, culture, and social justice.

J. Patrick Lannan, Jr., remembered well his father's unrealized desire that the foundation have a "plan." He knew that to make a meaningful success of the newly endowed foundation, he—along with his sisters Sharon Ferrill and Patricia Lawler and their cousin John R. Lannan— would have to create a set of goals and a system by which to achieve them. He began by asking four individuals to advise him and to serve as special advisers to the foundation's board: Gifford Phillips, a distinguished philanthropist, art collector, and trustee of The Museum of Modern Art, New York; John Elderfield, a curator at that same institution; James G. Butler, a distinguished Los Angeles attorney and self-educated literary scholar; and Dr. Paul Cummings, a progressive educator and founder of the Crossroads School for the Arts, Santa Monica.

The family and their new advisers decided to divide the foundation's activities into segments: grant programs for contemporary visual art and literature, and the collection. Over the past fourteen years, the foundation has had notable successes in each of these areas. With its Grants in the Visual Arts, Lannan Foundation has supported numerous shows in museums, exhibition facilities, and alternative spaces across the country. Typically it has provided assistance to projects that, due to their cutting-edge, even

FIGURE 2 J. Patrick Lannan, Jr., Sharon Lannan Ferrill, and Art Institute director James N. Wood, with Alberto Giacometti's *Tall Figure* (1947; bronze, h. 202 cm [79½ in.]; Gift of Lannan Foundation, 1959.21), 1987. The sculpture was given to the Art Institute by J. Patrick Lannan, Sr., in 1959.

provocative nature, might have difficulty finding other sponsorship. In addition the foundation has funded publications such as *Theories and Documents of Contemporary Art: A Sourcebook of Artists' Writings,* edited by Kristine Stiles and Peter Selz (Berkeley, 1996), as well as certain endeavors that exist outside an institutional context, notably James Turrell's ongoing Roden Crater project, which involves the carving and drilling of tunnels to admit light into an extinct volcano near Flagstaff, Arizona.

The foundation's literary program has proceeded with similar priorities and positive results. The Lannan Literary Awards provide substantial financial assistance to established writers of poetry, fiction, and nonfiction; the literary program also presents the "readings & conversations" events in association with SITE Santa Fe, and produces videotapes that document the series. Most recently the foundation inaugurated a Cultural Freedom Prize to recognize those "whose courageous work celebrates the human right to freedom of imagination, inquiry, and expression."

While these initiatives in grant-making and programming were getting under way in the late 1980s, the board also had to address the foundation's third area of focus—the art collection. To define the collection's mission and purpose, the foundation returned to one of J. Patrick Lannan, Sr.'s, primary goals: to help emerging and underrecognized artists. In 1987 the board decided to consolidate all of the foundation's operations in Los Angeles. Following that decision, the foundation closed the Lake Worth museum and in 1989 gave the facility to the Palm Beach Community College. The foundation renovated an industrial building in West Los Angeles to house administrative offices, exhibition galleries, a storage facility, and a library. In 1992 the foundation commissioned the artist Siah Armajani to design *The Poetry Garden* (now re-created at Beloit College, Beloit, Wisconsin), which served as a quiet, contemplative retreat for visitors and as a site for special events such as readings and lectures. In its new galleries, the foundation displayed selections from its collection and works borrowed from other collections, and also hosted temporary exhibitions organized by other institutions. Nineteen special exhibitions took place at this facility between 1990, when the foundation opened it, and 1996, when it closed. In these exhibitions, the foundation consistently sought to showcase significant work that might not otherwise have been seen in southern California; among the most impressive were Richter's *18 October 1977* series; a two-part presentation of "Photography in Contemporary German Art, 1960 to the Present"; "Robert Frank: Moving Out"; "Bill Viola: Stations"; and a number of significant exhibitions featuring West Coast artists.

The board also made a series of significant decisions regarding the collection's future augmentation. Two professional directors—first Bonnie Clearwater, who had worked for the Mark Rothko Foundation, New York, and then Lisa Lyons, who had been a curator at the Walker Art Center, Minneapolis—were hired to manage the foundation's art grant program, organize exhibitions, and build the collection.

Lannan Foundation was committed to collecting works by new and emerging artists. However, the board and its advisers realized that they could support younger artists not only by purchasing their work but also by maintaining holdings of acknowledged importance that lent distinction to the collection as a whole. In other words, lesser-known artists would benefit by association with more established individuals. Thus, the foundation continued to augment its core group of contemporary masterpieces in the 1990s, adding such outstanding pieces as Richter's *Woman Descending the Staircase* (p. 29) and his *Ice* paintings (p. 69–71), Nauman's *Clown Torture*, and Close's *Alex*. These works, together with the great Abstract Expressionist canvases, color-field paintings, and Minimalist objects assembled by J. Patrick Lannan, Sr., made the foundation's collection comparable in range and depth to that of a fine contemporary museum.

The foundation also purchased major works by emerging and underrecognized artists, moving with both an art museum's conceptual rigor and a private collector's adventurous spirit and substantial resources. Arguably, it was through this activity that the foundation exerted its greatest influence upon the contemporary art world. Casting its net widely, the foundation sought examples by international figures such as Jaar and Ruff, as well as New York–based artists such as Lynn Davis, Jackie Ferrara, and Kiki Smith. This worldwide roster notably included many artists working in California: the foundation obtained major pieces by Kelley, Charles Ray, and Ruppersberg; added examples by more established figures such as Robert Irwin and Edward Ruscha; and assembled significant bodies of work by Wallace Berman, Chris Burden, and John Miller. In many instances, the foundation in effect committed itself to individual artists, acquiring a number of works as their careers developed. Through the first half of the 1990s, public institutions and private individuals alike looked to Lannan Foundation for leadership in collecting contemporary art; artists and their dealers looked to it for support of work that was untested, risky, and often controversial.

The foundation's art and literary programs reflected the board's intention to concentrate its activities in areas that had been of primary interest to J. Patrick Lannan, Sr. His concern for social justice, however, had yet to be addressed. In 1994 the foundation answered this imperative by initiating the Indigenous Communities Program, which funds projects in rural Native American communities in the areas of education, indigenous cultures, the revival and preservation of languages, legal rights, traditional culture and education, environmental protection, and advocacy. The program's most ambitious projects are the construction of the Sinte Gleska University campus on the Rosebud Sioux Indian Reservation, South Dakota; the preservation of land and culture on behalf of the Independent Traditional Seminole Nation; and support for the creation of the Intertribal Sinkyone Wilderness Area in Mendocino, California.

By 1995 Lannan Foundation supported a large facility and staff in Los Angeles, an exhibition series, a generous grants program, an art-acquisition program, various literary activities, and its Indigenous Communities Program. Despite the substantial bequest of J. Patrick Lannan, Sr., board members felt that the foundation's resources were stretched, a problem to which they responded in three stages. First, they put a halt to the art-acquisition program. Then, more radically, they announced their intention to disperse the collection through a combination of sale and gift. Finally, they decided to close their West Los Angeles facility and move the foundation's headquarters to Santa Fe, New Mexico.

There were several reasons for these changes. Although the foundation's collecting activities were tremendously influential within the art world, J. Patrick Lannan, Jr., and the board found the collection's impact upon a wider public to be insufficient. They had hoped that museums around the country would borrow objects from the foundation for display with their own holdings and for inclusion in temporary exhibitions; while such loan requests did occur, there were fewer than had been expected. Works were therefore accumulating in storage without being seen. Exhibition attendance at the West Los Angeles facility was also disappointing.

Lannan Foundation's decisions to stop purchasing art and to disperse the collection were controversial, to say the least. Many in the arts community felt that younger artists were losing a unique and desperately needed resource; some argued that the foundation was breaking faith with certain artists and their representatives who had facilitated its acquisition of key works on the understanding that they would remain part of the distinguished Lannan Collection.

Painstakingly assembled bodies of work by individual artists might be separated, lessening their collective impact.

The foundation answered these objections by offering the collection exclusively to public institutions, reasoning that the works would attain greater visibility in museums around the country than they had had in the West Los Angeles galleries or in storage. In effect the foundation's strategy may be compared to that of J. Patrick Lannan, Sr., who eliminated divisions of his newly acquired companies in order to focus on a core capacity. The foundation identified as its prime mission the awarding of gifts and grants, and opted to support artists and museums through these means.

There is no question that The Art Institute of Chicago, the Museum of Contemporary Art, Los Angeles, and the Museum of Contemporary Art, Chicago, benefited handsomely from the foundation's decision, as did twenty-nine other museums. Following the closure of the West Los Angeles facility, the foundation issued grants to a number of institutions; as of this writing, however, the foundation has temporarily suspended its grant-making, as it evaluates ways to more effectively support past and future grant recipients.

Other cultural initiatives are nonetheless under way. In 1998 the foundation inaugurated a series of exhibitions at its new Santa Fe facility; thus far the presentations have included selected objects recently added to or remaining in the foundation's holdings, and art produced through a new artist-residency program. The foundation has also begun a new acquisition program in which it acquires works by an individual artist, displays them in the galleries and offices, and then offers them as gifts to a museum. In these and other ways, Lannan Foundation remains actively involved with contemporary art, and continues to support the public institutions that share its concerns. The programs and even the mission of Lannan Foundation will doubtless continue to evolve over time. Through its generous gift to The Art Institute of Chicago, however, an essential part of its history will remain fixed and visible.

Highlights of the Lannan Collection

Entries were written by the following individuals. Their entries are signed with their initials. All are associated with The Art Institute of Chicago.

A.D.B. Andrea D. Barnwell, *MacArthur Fellow, Department of Twentieth-Century Painting and Sculpture*

S.D. Stephanie D'Alessandro, *Andrew W. Mellon Postdoctoral Curatorial Fellow, Department of Twentieth-Century Painting and Sculpture*

R.H.D. Raymond Hernández-Durán, *MacArthur Fellow, Department of Prints and Drawings*

M.P. Mark Pascale, *Associate Curator, Department of Prints and Drawings*

J.E.R. James E. Rondeau, *Associate Curator of Contemporary Art, Department of Twentieth-Century Painting and Sculpture*

D.S. Daniel Schulman, *Associate Curator, Department of Twentieth-Century Painting and Sculpture*

S.S. Stephanie Skestos, *Curatorial Assistant, Department of Twentieth-Century Painting and Sculpture*

J.S. Jeremy Strick, *former Frances and Thomas Dittmer Curator of Twentieth-Century Painting and Sculpture*

C.W. Colin Westerbeck, *Associate Curator, Department of Photography*

Wall Painting with Stripes, 1944

Oil on canvas; 137.5 x 170.5 cm (54³⁄₁₆ x 67³⁄₁₆ in.) [see p. 92]

Both a scholar and painter, Robert Motherwell was a pivotal member of the group of Abstract Expressionists who came to artistic maturity just after World War II. While taking graduate art-history courses at Columbia University, New York, and painting independently at home, Motherwell was advised by his art-history professor Meyer Schapiro to apprentice himself to Kurt Seligmann, one of the cohort of Surrealist artists who had fled Europe for New York in the wake of the fall of France in 1940. Through Seligmann, Motherwell quickly became acquainted with a range of emigré artists and intellectuals, including André Breton, Marcel Duchamp, Max Ernst, Roberto Matta, and Yves Tanguy. The young Motherwell not only acted as a guide for these displaced Europeans, but sought to expose like-minded Americans to the work of European masters now in New York. Motherwell and his friends William Baziotes, Jackson Pollock, and others gathered on several occasions in Matta's studio to experiment with Surrealist creative practices such as automatic drawing and other techniques involving chance and intuition. Over the course of 1943–44, Peggy Guggenheim, the American dealer, collector, and then wife of Ernst, launched the careers of Baziotes, Pollock, and Motherwell, giving them their first one-person shows at her New York gallery, Art of This Century.

Of all the New York School painters, Motherwell aligned himself most closely with modern European art and literature, and his early works—made from about 1942 to 1947—exhibit a remarkable balance of modernist and Surrealist tendencies. *Wall Painting with Stripes* in particular fuses the geometric rigor found in the art of Henri Matisse, Piet Mondrian, and Pablo Picasso with an organic or biomorphic abstract language that is reminiscent of the imagery employed by Ernst and Joan Miró. (Scholars have long noted the striking similarities between *Wall Painting with Stripes* and Matisse's *Bathers by a River* [fig. 1], which was on view in a New York gallery in the early 1940s.)

Although signed and dated 1944, *Wall Painting with Stripes* shows signs of having been altered over time by the artist.[1] Pentimenti—evidence of previous compositions— are visible underneath the vertical bands of ocher and white paint. Motherwell simplified complex networks of lines into the egg-shaped forms and bulging curves now plainly visible. In some areas, the thinner, less juicy top layer cracked, owing to the different speeds at which fat and thin paint dries.[2] The active and weathered quality of the surface gives *Wall Painting* a false patina of age, suggesting that the work was created by forces beyond those of the individual artist—that it is actually a "wall painting." *Wall Painting* is also significant because, with its large scale and its formal vocabulary of arcs and straight lines, it heralds the signature imagery that Motherwell realized most fully in the *Spanish Elegies*, the series of monumental works he initiated in 1948. **D. S.**

FIGURE 1 Henri Matisse (French; 1869–1954). *Bathers by a River*, 1909, 1913, and 1916. Oil on canvas; 259.7 x 389.9 cm (102½ x 153½ in.). The Art Institute of Chicago, Charles H. and Mary F. S. Worcester Collection (1953.158).

Figure, 1946

Georgia marble; 168.3 x 49.5 x 38.1 cm (66¼ x 19½ x 15 in.) [see p. 93]

In 1946 Isamu Noguchi carved *Figure*, a gray-and-white, life-sized marble sculpture composed of intersecting, planar units. That same year, The Museum of Modern Art, New York, featured similar abstracted sculptures by Noguchi in a group show, "Fourteen Americans." The exhibition marked a new direction for the artist, who had been known until then primarily for his portraits. Inspired in part by the elegant, reductive carvings of his mentor, the Romanian sculptor Constantin Brancusi, and by the evocative, biomorphic shapes that had become a hallmark of Surrealism, these new works earned Noguchi critical praise. In a statement in the show's catalogue, he articulated his desire to produce work that mediated against the destruction of World War II, offering significance in a post-war world that seemed devoid of meaning. "The essence of sculpture," he wrote, "is for me the perception of space, the continuum of existence. . . . Our knowledge of the universe has filled space with energy, driving us toward a greater chaos and new equilibriums. . . . It is the sculptor who orders and animates space, gives it meaning."[1] The sense of universality that the artist—whose father was Japanese and mother American—hoped to achieve can be seen in the Art Institute's *Figure*.

Noguchi invested *Figure* with a sense of timelessness by referencing *kouroi*, archaic Greek stone sculptures of standing male youths (he even entitled the first of many such pieces *Kouros* [1944; New York, The Metropolitan Museum of Art]). With its weight equally distributed on two "legs," one of which is planted at a right angle to the massive plane behind it, the sculpture stands quietly and confidently, echoing the still, enigmatic poses of *kouroi*. The vertical element emerging at an angle from the oval aperture near the top of *Figure* echoes a *kouros*'s gently raised forearm. Beyond formal similarities, *Figure* and its Greek antecedents share symbolic aspects. Evoking the heroic, generative power of youth, the ancient statues served as steles, or grave markers. Perhaps Noguchi intended *Figure* and related sculptures to function as witnesses and antidotes to death and destruction. The work's elegant forms and cool, polished surface indeed suggest a state of transcendence and transformation, while its self-containment evokes a kind of existential isolation in an era of upheaval.

At the time Noguchi made *Figure*, he was involved in several projects that extended beyond his activity as a sculptor but contributed significantly to it. Between 1944 and 1950, he produced a number of theatrical sets for the mythology-inspired work of modern dancer Martha Graham and her company. The skeletonlike elements he designed in 1945 for Graham's "Herodiade," for example, are organic in form and flexible in construction; like *Figure*, they connote the human form and invite meditation on mortality. Noguchi expressed his desire to evoke in these sets "the desecration of beauty, the consciousness of time."[2]

In 1943 Noguchi had also become involved with furniture design. *Figure* consists of four discrete, carved pieces: one large element, punctuated with curvilinear and rectilinear openings and depressions, and three sections that hang or slide into place and are held there by gravity. This construction recalls a traditional kind of furniture making that had been revived in modern times by such designers as Americans Greene and Greene and the Dutch, De Stijl artist Gerrit Rietveld. Noguchi's furniture, which was manufactured and sold by the Herman Miller Company, reveals a love of simple construction and natural materials reflected in Asian art and architecture, as well as the streamlined look of modernist industrial design, as embodied in the *Dymaxion Car* (1931) designed by the sculptor's friend R. Buckminster Fuller or in Kem Weber's self-assembly *Airline Chair* (1934–35). Thus linking the classical with the atomic age, *Figure* may be considered the embodiment of the post-nuclear "new man." For Noguchi all of these sources helped him return to the elemental—in meaning, materials, and construction—as a way to begin anew after a time of destruction and chaos. **S. D.**

FIGURE 1 Isamu Noguchi assembling *Avatar* (Otterlo, Rijksmuseum Kröller-Müller) for "Abstract and Surrealist Art," The Art Institute of Chicago, 1947.

Sam Francis (AMERICAN; 1923–1994)

In Lovely Blueness, 1955–56

Oil on canvas; 309.9 x 365.8 cm (122 x 144 in.) [see p. 89]

S am Francis's monumental canvas *In Lovely Blueness* evokes the sensation of standing at the threshold of a vast and boundless space that seems to expand and contract as if it were a living organism. Large areas of thinly applied white paint, frosted with streaks of lavender, cover most of the surface. These fluffy shapes float and converge, suspended in a loose matrix of scumbled bursts and spattered rivulets of transparent, prismatic colors: red, yellow, orange, and blue. At approximately ten by twelve feet, this painting was one of Francis's largest works to date; it inaugurated, in the late 1950s, a succession of even larger, intensely lyrical, and critically acclaimed paintings. Airy, expansive, and exuberant, these works are informed by a variety of artistic sources, including Abstract Expressionism and early twentieth-century French art.

Francis began to paint in earnest during a long period of convalescence from the grave injuries that he suffered in an airplane accident while he was training as a pilot in World War II. Largely immobilized for months, constrained to lie on his back or stomach, Francis later said that he "probably would have died if it had not been for painting."[1] After his recovery, he completed a degree in painting at the University of California, Berkeley. Although far from New York, the San Francisco Bay Area was hardly provincial in these years: visiting teachers such as Hans Hofmann, Mark Rothko, and Clyfford Still (see p. 20) exposed students like Francis to New York School abstraction. After Francis graduated in 1950, he bypassed New York altogether, going directly to Europe on a GI Bill stipend.

Living in Paris for most of the 1950s, Francis quickly developed a unique, hybrid manner, characterized in part by a merging of the two main strains of Abstract Expressionism: on the one hand, the gestural, calligraphic, and energetic brushwork of Jackson Pollock and Willem de Kooning; and, on the other, the strong emphasis on color harmony of Rothko, Still, and Barnett Newman. At the same time, Francis incorporated lessons learned from the late Impressionist works of Claude Monet and Paul Cézanne, as well as their twentieth-century followers Pierre Bonnard and Henri Matisse. In 1953 the Orangerie reopened in Paris, giving many visitors, including Francis, their first experience of Monet's astonishing *Water Lilies*, mural decorations that condense and collapse views of sky and garden on an ever-changing, reflective surface of water. Francis's encounter with these expansive, lyrical, and virtually abstract works proved an essential component of his artistic education.

In Lovely Blueness is one of two paintings with that title that Francis made between 1955 and 1957. The Art Institute's canvas, probably the first of the two, was acquired by J. Patrick Lannan, Sr., in 1959, after it was shown in several West Coast museums. The other, even larger version is now in the collection of the Musée national d'art moderne, Paris. Francis, who was often inspired by literary works and kept a notebook containing titles of books and verses, named these paintings after a poem by the German Romantic writer Friedrich Hölderlin. "In Lovely Blueness," which touches on many issues of art, nature, and identity, begins with the author gazing into the sky:

In lovely blue the steeple blossoms
With its metal roof. Around which
Drift swallow cries, around which
Lies most loving blue.[2]

D. S.

Jay DeFeo (AMERICAN; 1929–1989)

The Annunciation, 1957–59

Oil on canvas; 306.7 x 189.2 cm (120¾ x 74½ in.) [see p. 89]

The eccentric, visionary artist Jay DeFeo ceaselessly challenged the artistic standards and trends of her time. Although she received little national attention during her career, she had a momentous influence on San Francisco Bay Area artists, such as Bruce Connor, Craig Kauffman, and Ed Moses, and on the California Beat and Funk art movements of the 1950s and 1960s.

In 1951, after earning a degree in painting from the University of California, Berkeley, DeFeo won a prestigious fellowship to study in Spain, France, Italy, and North Africa. While abroad, she became intrigued by prehistoric and Renaissance art; and the painter Sam Francis (see p. 16), with whom she had studied in California and then visited in Paris, exposed her to Abstract Expressionism. Upon her return to the United States in 1953, DeFeo stopped in New York to view the work of Philip Guston and other New York School artists. She then went back to California, where she executed her first monumental, Abstract Expressionist compositions. She immersed herself in the Beat movement that was evolving in San Francisco, and associated with artists, poets, and jazz musicians who strove to unite the intuitive and intellectual components of creative activity.[1] In 1959 DeFeo was included—along with Johns, Kelly, Nevelson, Rauschenberg, and Stella—in the important "Sixteen Americans" exhibition, held at The Museum of Modern Art, New York. She continued to show her paintings in several West Coast galleries until 1963, when she withdrew completely from the commercial art scene to concentrate on the completion of a legendary, colossal painting, entitled *The Rose* (1958–66; San Francisco Art Institute).

In *The Annunciation*—a large-scale composition depicting a winged torso suggestive of an angel—white, feathery brush strokes, overlaid with brown, blue, and silvery tones, ascend into a dark background. DeFeo used a palette knife to apply thick paint across the canvas, creating a dense surface texture. While her working method was expressive and spontaneous, it was also highly controlled and restrained: she spent months, and even years, reworking and building up the surfaces of her compositions. Like many of her paintings, *The Annunciation* is explosive and volcanic, while retaining an aura of vulnerability and fragility.

In 1959 the artist described *The Annunciation* in a letter to J. Patrick Lannan, Sr., in a way that underscores the universal yet intensely personal spiritual themes invoked in her paintings of the mid-to-late 1950s:

I painted this kind of winged vision which announces in my eyes or promises some realization of all that is good in this existence, and more specifically it is a promise to me of the realization of certain powers creatively—and when I say that, I make some association between the words creative and spiritual or divine. Or at least I feel this way when I am doing my best. . . . I don't choose such titles with any narrow Christian interpretation in mind. It doesn't have to do with any specific religion at all. It is only a symbol. I have to make my own philosophy or religion in my life and I'm too young to understand it as yet.[2]

S. S.

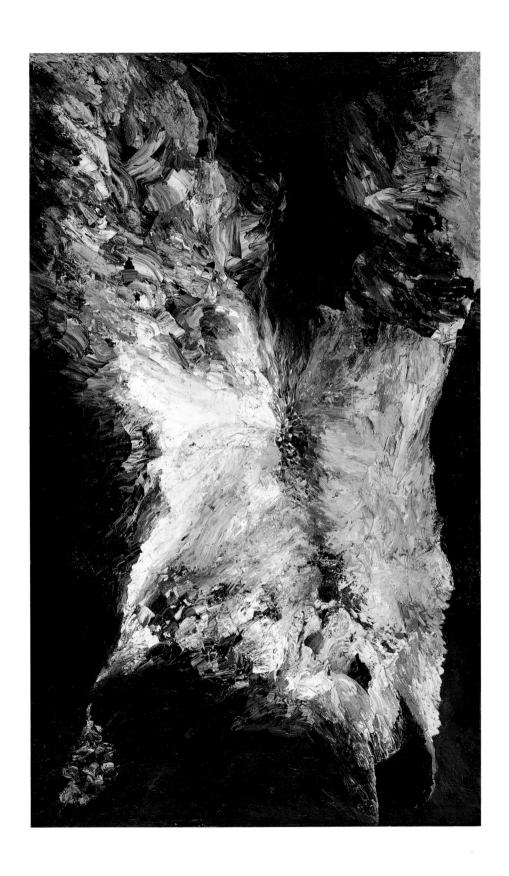

Untitled, 1958

Oil on canvas; 292.2 x 406.4 cm (114¼ x 160 in.) [see p. 97]

n the late 1940s, Clyfford Still, along with Barnett Newman and Mark Rothko, originated the type of Abstract Expressionism known as "Field Painting," a term used to describe very large canvases dominated by one uniform color or by a few colors closely related in hue and value. In comparison to Newman's incandescent expanses of undifferentiated color divided by beams and "zips," and Rothko's juxtapositions of luminous bands of floating color, Still's work—with its stark and brutal paint surfaces—struck many as the most radical and unruly.

Still considered his grandiose abstractions to be extensions of his identity and records of his emotional life. No major American artist guarded his legacy more zealously than Still. On the rare occasions he exhibited during his lifetime, he exerted complete control over the presentation of his works. He generously gave museums in Buffalo and San Francisco a large number of paintings, but he sold only a handful of works to collectors and other museums; today the great majority of his oeuvre remains in his estate, out of public view. More than twenty years after his death, Still's art continues to evoke shock and wonder.

We experience the monumentally scaled *Untitled*, like most of Still's mature work, as a sheer wall of paint—imposing and self-sustaining, making no concessions to conventional notions of beauty or pictorial illusionism. In contrast to Newman and Rothko, who usually applied paint thinly and uniformly, Still subjected his materials to extreme, almost sculptural manipulation. This painting's textural effects give it an insistent, complex materiality. Dominated by blacks that the artist applied with both a trowel and brushes, the surface is by turns reflective and chalky, granular and smooth, feathery and leaden. These variegated black surfaces are even more emphatic because their continuity is broken by areas of blank canvas and white paint. Like veins in igneous rock, streaks of orange, yellow, and green paint are embedded in the black voids. Mediating between the light and dark masses are areas of alizarin crimson, heightened at the edges, as if enflamed, by bright orange. *Untitled*, which sustains a dramatic equilibrium between light and dark, joins one other monumental work by Still in the Art Institute, *1951-52* (1951–52), one of the artist's few almost completely black paintings.

Born in 1904 in a remote town in North Dakota and raised in Spokane, Washington, and rural Alberta, Canada, Still spent most of his career far from New York; in the 1930s and 1940s, he taught in Washington State and San Francisco, and, in his later years, lived in rural Maryland. As is the case with Jackson Pollock (who, when queried about whether he painted from nature, responded famously: "I am nature"), a mythic identity of rugged, western individualism clings to Still. The unconventionally crude, jagged forms in his paintings have prompted comparisons to the sublime mode of Romantic landscape painting. Still's uniquely inspired vision is not unlike that of nineteenth-century English artist J. M. W. Turner, who worked essentially in isolation and demanded to be regarded as unique among his peers. **D. S.**

Abstract Painting 1960–1965, 1960–65

Oil on canvas; 152.4 x 152.4 cm (60 x 60 in.) [see p. 93]

After experimenting with color and gesture in various abstract and expressionist styles during the 1940s and early 1950s, Ad Reinhardt renounced color in 1953 and began to produce only black paintings. From 1960 until his death seven years later, Reinhardt painted exclusively on canvases with identical, black compositions and sixty-inch square formats. The artist made these extreme choices in order to transcend ordinary cognitive experiences of art and life. He hoped, as he stated, to "push painting beyond its thinkable, seeable, feelable limits."[1]

A first glance at *Abstract Painting 1960–1965* might prompt us to think that Reinhardt's goal was to achieve imperceptivity. The painting's surface—opaquely, densely, and insistently black—seems to reject viewing. However, if we continue to look at the work, we will notice in time that the black is not as impenetrable as it first appears: there are variations within it, as well as two areas with ethereal passages of blue. The canvas is trisected horizontally and vertically by subtly hued bands, gossamer layers of pigment that overlap and float delicately within the indeterminate depth of the painting.

Abstract Painting 1960–1965 requires a kind of observation that is slow, focused, and contemplative in an almost spiritual sense. In fact the painting's intersecting bands create a pattern that can be read as either a mandala or a cross. Reinhardt studied Asian art and philosophy, traveled throughout the Near and Far East, and taught Asian art history at both Brooklyn and Hunter Colleges in New York. While both the mandala and cross typically function as conduits to reflection, Reinhardt did not intend this painting to refer to a specific religious belief. Rather, he used these forms to invoke the inner concentration and spiritual rewards that can occur in an extended and profound experience of works of art.

Reinhardt's work not only asks its viewers to take the time to reflect upon it, but its precise patterning and elusive effects demanded an involved, exacting, and lengthy process on the part of its maker. The rigor of Reinhardt's enterprise is revealed in his painstaking methods. Rejecting a "hard-edge" style, he preferred to paint edges by hand, feeling that a taped line would produce a visibly ridged surface. Using a one-inch-wide brush, he obliterated the traces of his hand until the canvas had attained an allover surface of shallow, deliberate, and almost rhythmically applied strokes. Moreover, the artist placed his canvases on low tables and bent far over them, painting in a physically demanding—almost prostrate—position. Thus, Reinhardt's creative process represented an act of balance, focus, and fortitude similar to that of the most rigorous meditation. **S. D.**

Mouth (Mund), 1963
Oil on canvas; 67.3 x 74.3 cm (26½ x 29¼ in.) [see p. 93]

Gerhard Richter included *Mouth* in his first two public exhibitions, both held in Düsseldorf in 1963. The first of these, a group show, was organized with fellow students from the Düsseldorf Akademie, Manfred Kuttner, Konrad Lueg, and Sigmar Polke (see p. 50). The second, more famous event—as much a performance, or "action," as an exhibition—took place one evening at a furniture store. Richter and Lueg (who later became a prominent art dealer under the name Konrad Fischer) placed sofas, chairs, and other furniture upon low pedestals. The artists then sat on the furniture, turning themselves into objects of display. Several paintings by Lueg and Richter, among them *Mouth*, were included in the exhibition, which was titled "Living with Pop—A Demonstration for Capitalist Realism."

Mouth typifies Richter's concerns in his earliest Pop, or "capitalist realism," phase. Beginning in 1962, the artist derived images for his so-called Photo Paintings from photographs he found: anonymous snapshots, postcards, and pages from newspapers and magazines. At first he conspicuously altered or manipulated these images, or placed them in a non-photographic pictorial framework.[1] He derived *Mouth* from a photograph of the French actress Brigitte Bardot, radically cropping the image so that her lips and mouth are isolated and disembodied.

Although Richter did not identify Bardot as his subject in the painting's title, his choice of pictorial source is nonetheless significant.[2] Bardot—who figures in a later Richter painting, *Mother and Daughter (B.)* (1965; Oberhausen, Städtische Galerie)—was perhaps the most celebrated European sex symbol of her day. She exemplified the emerging nexus of sex and mass culture that fascinated American and European Pop artists alike. Isolating and exaggerating Bardot's famously sensual mouth, Richter created an image at once humorous and disturbing. On display along with other commodities in the furniture store during Richter's "capitalist realism" demonstration, this disembodied image may well have suggested the peculiar alienation of mass-marketed sexuality.

By late 1963, Richter had adopted a less distorting manner of transposing his photographic sources. Perhaps this stylistic evolution prompted him to destroy several of his earlier paintings; he would have destroyed *Mouth* too, had he not already given it to his colleague Kuttner. In a 1993 interview, Richter noted that *Mouth* was a painting he had come to hate, feeling that it was "too much Pop art," and disliking the "surrealistic" isolation and deformation of the face and mouth. Examining a photograph of the painting during the interview, however, Richter revised his negative opinion: He now found the painting "interesting" and "O.K.," a very good "document" of his early work and beginnings in Pop Art.[3] J. S.

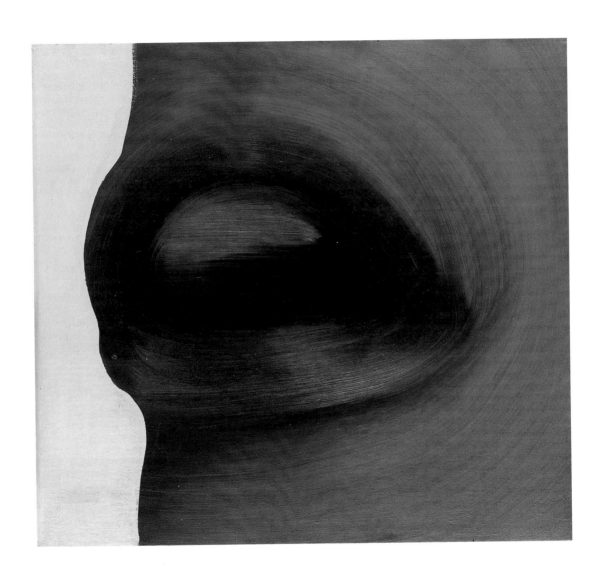

Richard Artschwager (AMERICAN; BORN 1924)

Table with Pink Tablecloth, 1964

Formica on wood; 64.8 x 111.8 x 111.8 cm (25½ x 44 x 44 in.) [see p. 86]

While Richard Artschwager's work is wide-ranging in its materials and techniques, it is always iconoclastic. It includes rubberized hair cubes, oversized elliptical objects made of wood and bristles called *blps*, grisaille photographic paintings on Celotex, and most recently mysteriously shaped packing-crate sculptures. Artschwager first attracted attention as a maker of furniture surrogates, drawing upon his experience as the owner of a successful carpentry and furniture-design business. Before this he had trained as a scientist, worked as an intelligence officer in World War II, and eked out a living photographing babies. He had drawn and painted sporadically in his youth, but he did not become a professional artist until relatively late in life. Distanced as they seem from the process of making art, Artschwager's life experiences all contributed to shaping his works into inquisitive, cerebrally potent, witty, and ultimately enigmatic ruminations on the nature of perception.

Artschwager's first solo exhibition took place at the Leo Castelli Gallery, New York, in 1965 (he was forty-one years old). The works in this show, including *Table with Pink Tablecloth*, can all be characterized as compact, geometric masses wrapped with formica "pictures" to resemble domestic items. Some critics initially labeled Artschwager's chairs, pianos, and dressers as Pop Art, because of their derivation from the utilitarian and incorporation of commercial materials; others saw them as Minimalist, because of their geometric, solid forms and objectlike presence. Neither classification, nor others applied later, such as Conceptual Art or Photo-Realism, adequately defines the aims of an artist who has consistently attempted to reveal the levels of deception involved in pictorial illusionism.

Artschwager described *Table with Pink Tablecloth* as "the way a table with a tablecloth is in a painting, in a still life—a three-dimensional still life."[1] Substituting formica for pigment, the artist constructed *Table* with flat, plastic surfaces that mimic a pink, speckled cloth; a tan wooden table top and legs; and even a shadowy space underneath. The work asks us to understand the formica as both mass and void, a kind of three-dimensional musing on perception that has an art-historical antecedent in Georges Braque's fake-texture, Cubist collages. However, the sculpture's material, formica, was used extensively after World War II for commercial products rather than works of art. Playing with these associations, *Table with Pink Tablecloth* stubbornly refuses illusionism and nostalgically evokes post-war luncheonette counters and other non-art uses. Tension is created as well in the disjunction between the essential character of a table and this particular "table." Indeed, Artschwager's "table" has been transmuted from the painted world into the sculptural realm. In that translation, it has lost much of its function and essential character. While it looks like a table, it is too low to be useful and too solid to pull a chair underneath. It is in effect no longer a table but rather a three-dimensional evocation of one. Artschwager had initially intended such constructions to sit in homes alongside other furnishings as a way to give tangible reality to the flat, illusionistic world of painting and to bring artistic artifice, as well as the slippery slope of perception, into sharp relief. This is an idea he later abandoned, perhaps recognizing that the works in themselves achieved these goals.[2] **S. D.**

Woman Descending the Staircase (Frau die Treppe herabgehend), 1965

Oil on canvas; 200.7 x 129.5 cm (79 x 51 in.) [see p. 94]

The aesthetic territory that Gerhard Richter explored in his Photo Paintings (see p. 24) of the mid- and late 1960s tended to the assertively mundane. Most of these canvases reproduce such apparently ordinary images as anonymous family snapshots and insignificant newspaper clippings. An image of an undistinguished building facade, or even a simple wooden chair, acquires an odd fascination when painted by Richter, although the artist in no way suggested that the original object or image is anything other than ordinary. In this context, *Woman Descending the Staircase* is exceptional, distinguished by the elegance of the subject; the formality and drama of the composition; and even the work's glossy, silver-blue brushwork. This may be Richter's most glamorous painting.

These qualities encourage speculation about the woman's identity, which remains unknown. *Woman Descending the Staircase* is not, however, a celebrity portrait. More typological than individual, the work addresses the way photography and painting create impressions of beauty, elegance, and glamor.

In *Atlas*—the compendium of photographic images Richter has assembled over nearly four decades, and from which he has derived many of his paintings—the source image for *Woman Descending the Staircase* is placed next to that for another painting, *Secretary* (see fig. 1).[1] The two are virtual pendants. The sturdy secretary, wearing a frumpy skirt and blouse, strides briskly past an office door, while the alluring subject of *Woman Descending the Staircase*, dressed in glimmering sheath and flowing scarf, seems almost to float down the stairs, her every motion a public gesture. The juxtaposition of these two images suggests how women's appearance, dress, and gesture call forth notions of beauty, class, and different types of public spheres.

Comparing *Woman Descending the Staircase* to its photographic source further underscores the artist's aims. Relative to the photograph, the artist broadened the proportions of the painting; widened the staircase and turned it slightly toward the viewer; and eliminated the stair carpet and details of the wall moldings. As a result, the painting appears purer, grander, and more monumental than its photographic source. Painterly techniques add to this effect. In his early canvases, Richter typically applied dry brush strokes laterally across the top layer,

thereby obscuring his images; here, these strokes have a distinctive sheen that emphasizes the glistening highlights of the woman's dress and the reflections on the polished staircase. In this way, Richter transformed the already attractive original image into an icon of elegance.

Another source lurks behind Richter's *Woman Descending the Staircase*: Marcel Duchamp's famous early abstraction *Nude Descending a Staircase* (1912; Philadelphia Museum of Art). In a 1991 interview, Richter acknowledged his "unconscious antagonism" toward Duchamp's *Nude* and said that he had responded to it in his 1966 painting *Ema (Nude on a Staircase)* (Cologne, Museum Ludwig), for which his first wife served as model.[2] Certainly, *Ema* is explicit in its Duchampian reference, but it may be inspired as much by Richter's own, slightly earlier *Woman Descending the Staircase* as it was by Duchamp's masterpiece. The unadorned nudity and inward-turning gaze of the figure in *Ema* seems a deliberate contrast to the extreme of artifice and public display represented in *Woman*.

Richter's techniques of blurring lend to all of his Photo Paintings a sense of absence or loss that is especially poignant in *Woman Descending the Staircase*. Richter objected to Duchamp's *Nude Descending a Staircase* because he "could never accept that it had put paid [i.e., put an end], once and for all, to a certain kind of painting."[3] In *Woman Descending the Staircase*, Richter deployed all of his technical facility to convey the appeal of the kind of representation that Duchamp had obviated. The very beauty of his subject and his painting makes it an allegory for the desirability of representation. *Woman Descending the Staircase* seems to suggest that, in the wake of Duchamp, this desire is inevitably thwarted. **J. S.**

FIGURE 1 Newspaper clippings from Gerhard Richter's *Atlas*, 1964–67 (detail). Collection of the artist.

Explosion at Sea, 1966

Oil on canvas; 34.3 x 59.7 cm (13½ x 23½ in.) [see p. 86]

E xplosion at Sea represents a significant moment in the development of Vija Celmins's art. Celmins's early work depicts everyday objects with an emphasis on rendering three-dimensional forms two-dimensionally. While she produced these paintings in the wake of Pop Art, her interest in the quotidian had nothing to do with issues of commerce or the media but rather with the illusionistic process of image-making itself. Celmins's mature work depicts expansive atmospheric spaces, such as seascapes, in which no human-made forms are visible, and galaxies that evoke the mystery and glow of the universe. In their restricted palettes and meditative quality, Celmins's images relate more to the perceptually based Minimalism of Agnes Martin, although Martin's work has always been purely abstract.

In the mid-1960s, Celmins started to use photographs from books, magazines, and newspapers that she found in secondhand stores and at yard sales as the point of departure for her paintings. After locating a wealth of material on World War II—including photographs of guns; assorted disasters; and American, German, and Japanese war planes—the artist executed a number of paintings and sculptures on the themes of war, technology, and devastation. It is to this group of works that Explosion at Sea belongs.

The meticulous and time-consuming methods Celmins used to portray war have been compared to the painstaking efforts required to construct model airplanes.[1] In Explosion at Sea, a small, horizontal canvas, she employed subtle layers of precise brush strokes to construct a detailed image of an attack on an aircraft carrier.[2] As in most of the works in the series, Celmins created here a disturbing contrast between the intimacy of the format and brushwork and the haunting seriousness of the theme. Moreover, although the composition's careful detail links it to the vintage photographs that served as her sources, Celmins's exclusive use of thinly applied, austere, gray tonalities places the image at great remove from the violent realities of war.

Celmins's war series seems to be connected to her personal history.[3] As a child, she and her family were forced to flee their native Latvia when war threatened. After seeking refuge in Eastern Europe and then in West Germany, they arrived in the United States in 1949. Celmins explained,

"I generally think of my childhood as being full of excitement and magic, and terror, too—bombs, fires, fear, escape— very eventful. It wasn't 'till I was ten years old and living in the United States that I realized living with these images was not everyone's experience."[4] In works such as Explosion at Sea, Celmins's intense childhood experiences seem to have been given focus, filtered, and transformed by the precision and concentration of her artistic process. **A. D. B.**

Alfred Jensen (AMERICAN; BORN GUATEMALA, 1903–1981)

The Acroatic Rectangle, Per XIII, 1967
Oil on canvas; 182.9 x 149.9 cm (72 x 59 in.) [see p. 91]

[see p. 91]

Alfred Jensen's thickly painted, geometric compositions incorporate systems of numbers, symbols, and patterns drawn from the ancient and modern teachings of numerology, astronomy, and mythology. Although his work has been compared to that of the Constructivists, Abstract Expressionists, Minimalists, and Pop artists, Jensen deliberately remained on the fringe of prevailing artistic styles, and he was never comfortable identifying with the primary tenets of these movements.

Jensen was born in 1903 in Guatemala to a Danish father and a Polish-German mother. He trained at the School of Fine Art in San Diego, and in Munich with Hans Hofmann in 1926. Three years later, the patronage of an American art collector enabled Jensen to continue his education at the Académie scandinave in Paris, where the painter Charles Dufresne encouraged him to work in heavy impasto. For several years, Jensen traveled throughout Europe, visiting artists' studios and spending much of his time in museums, studying the art of the Old Masters. In the 1950s, he maintained a studio in New York, where he witnessed the burgeoning of the American avant-garde. He exhibited his paintings in New York at the Stable Gallery in 1955, along with work by Joseph Cornell, Willem de Kooning, Alan Kaprow, Claes Oldenburg, and Robert Rauschenberg.[1] Nonetheless, in an attempt to express himself individually, Jensen rejected current trends such as all-over painting, collage, and Pop subjects. He established his own style—thickly painted compositions of colorful, kaleidoscopic patterns—founded on mathematics, color theories, and science. Jensen's fascination with the human desire to understand universal truths led him to create highly calculated compositions that are tranquil and meditative and, at the same time, pulsating and expressive.

In 1964 Jensen spent six months in Egypt, France, and Greece. Over the next few years, he painted several large compositions inspired by his trip and by his study of ancient Greek architectural and numerical ratios.[2] The vibrant and richly textured *Acroatic Rectangle, Per XIII* is the largest and most ambitious of a series of eighteen *Acroatic Rectangle* paintings.[3] The title of the series derives from the Greek word *akroasis*, meaning a pinnacle, or a towering, pyramidal structure. Found in Aristotle's writings, the term "acroatic" also appears in *Akróasis*, a book published in Basel in 1964 by the philosopher and musicologist Dr. Hans Kayser.[4]

In the Art Institute's complex and highly systematic work, horizontal bands of white, black, green, burnt orange, and violet converge at the center of a rectangle, creating illusions of shifting planes that ascend and descend, while they simultaneously advance and retreat from the image's midpoint. *The Acroatic Rectangle, Per XIII*, like all of Jensen's paintings, acquires its formal effect through the artist's arcane, cross-cultural code of numerical and alphabetical symbols. It defies categorization, pushing at the boundaries of both illusionism and abstraction. **S. S.**

Gerhard Richter (GERMAN; BORN 1932)

Mrs. Wolleh with Children (Frau Wolleh mit Kindern), 1968

Oil on canvas; 200 x 160 cm (78¾ x 63 in.) [see p. 94]

The least sentimental of painters, Gerhard Richter has long evinced a paradoxical fascination with romantic subjects. As if systematically exploring a catalogue of exhausted, anachronistic motifs, Richter has painted landscapes, seascapes, candles, skulls, and flowers. Images of families and children too have been subject to the artist's scrutiny. Anonymous family snapshots provided the point of departure for several of his earliest paintings, while a photograph of Richter's own daughter, which he took himself, served as the basis for one of his most famous later works, *Betty* (1988; Saint Louis Art Museum). For *Mrs. Wolleh with Children*, Richter adapted a photograph made by his friend the photographer Lothar Wolleh of the latter's wife and children. Wolleh took the photograph in Richter's presence, and, when Richter completed the painting based upon it, he gave it to his friend (who eventually sold it).[1]

Formally, *Mrs. Wolleh with Children* is one of the most distinctive works in Richter's oeuvre. All of Richter's Photo Paintings (see p. 24) are blurred, an effect that distances his subjects and renders elusive even the most vivid images. In *Mrs. Wolleh with Children*, Richter carried this effect of blurring to an extreme. Only the broad outlines and most general features of the sitters are legible. The expression on Mrs. Wolleh's face is suggested, but remains enigmatic, while the faces of her two children are entirely indistinct.

Mrs. Wolleh with Children's color scheme is similarly unusual. Richter used local color relatively rarely in his Photo Paintings of the 1960s. Typically, he worked from black-and-white photographs, and his canvases accordingly feature a uniform tone and coloration. *Mrs. Wolleh with Children*, although not the only colored painting Richter produced during this period, is strikingly antinaturalistic. The artist placed the figures within a somewhat modulated rust-yellow field that offers no clue as to the setting. Mrs. Wolleh's long, black dress contrasts strongly with this ground, and even more with the ghostly whiteness of her apparently naked children. The overall blurring of detail, however, tends to flatten mother and children alike, turning them into a single outline or shape.

While the direct source of this painting was a photograph of specifically identified, contemporary individuals,

it is impossible to ignore references to a broader and more ancient iconography. Mrs. Wolleh's children clearly suggest cupids, but they also remind us of Renaissance images of the infant Jesus playing with Saint John. Mrs. Wolleh, standing in the midst of a vast atmospheric field, children at either side, recalls the figure of the Virgin in Titian's *Assumption* (c. 1540; Venice, Scuola di San Rocco), or paintings by Lucas Cranach of Venus and Cupid.

Richter has rarely made specific art-historical references in his work; two instances are *Ema (Nude on a Staircase)* of 1966 (Cologne, Museum Ludwig), and the five-panel series *Annunciation: After Titian* of 1973 (Schaffhausen, Hallen für neue Kunst; Italy, private collection). Nonetheless, the kind of vague allusion evident in *Mrs. Wolleh with Children* pervades much of the artist's work. This painting is, on the one hand, a personal document of friendship and a portrait of specific individuals, and, on the other, a general, depersonalized, and art-historically informed image of motherhood. Moreover, it offers a telling account of the ways in which representation conditions and literally clouds interpretation, aiding and frustrating it by turns. **J. S.**

9 Objects (9 Objekte), 1968

Nine photo-offset lithographs on paper; each 44.8 x 44.8 cm (17⅝ x 17⅝ in.) [see p. 94]

Gerhard Richter shares with Bruce Nauman a distinctly pluralistic pursuit of art, maintaining within his oeuvre continuity of approach rather than style. Richter's *9 Objects*, like Nauman's nearly contemporary *Studies for Holograms* (p. 40), raises important issues about the use of photography in art, and also about the nature of contemporary artistic printmaking. Richter considers his prints to be "antiprints," created to run counter to the concept of a print as a beautiful object;[1] something similar could be said about Nauman's *Studies for Holograms.* Both artists used photomechanical methods of reproducing images that had been staged specifically for the prints or for other projects. And, while artists as varied as Richard Hamilton, Robert Rauschenberg, and Andy Warhol had previously employed similar means to produce their printed work, none was as deadpan and seemingly artless as Richter and Nauman.

Richter created *9 Objects* six years after he began making his so-called Photo Paintings using appropriated photographs (see p. 24)—motivated, somewhat like Warhol, by the idea of removing the artist's hand or personality from the painted work. *9 Objects* is related to Richter's 1968 series of images of windows, *Shadow Pictures*, for which he initiated his own photographic model. The artist used the motif of a single form and its shadow in the painting *Shadow Picture 1* (Leverkusen, Städtisches Museum, long-term loan) and in two related collotype prints to explore the visual conundrum of figure and ground—the interplay between that which appears to sit on top or in front of the picture plane, and that which seems to recede into the illusionistic space of the picture. Through careful cropping and lighting, Richter seemed to imply that figure and ground might be positive or negative and that, despite the apparent verisimilitude of the figure and its shadow, the form of the shadow in no way agrees with that of the figure.

In Richter's most successful work, the tension is never resolved between reality and abstraction, between mechanical reproduction and painterly skill.[2] This tension informs *9 Objects.* Richter derived the offset images in this portfolio from photographs he took himself and then retouched.[3] The subjects are wooden, geometric objects that he transformed so that each shape represents a physical impossibility. The configurations of the nine "objects" undermine all sense of Euclidean geometry, according to which the visible part of a figure reliably indicates the form of its hidden parts. Plate h is difficult to read in much the same way that the *Shadow Pictures* are. The object apparently casts a logical shadow and rests firmly on a textured floor, but the combination of blurred, manipulated ground and the impossible joinery of the object's corners yields conflicting readings, so that the object seems to be hovering and/or toppling over, depending on the viewer's perspective. Plates b, c, and d read like Sol LeWitt sculptures run amok.[4] Plates e and g appear to comment on the pedagogical exercise of drawing an open, three-dimensional form—like a chair—in space as a means of learning one-point perspective. In plate g, the "object" sits in an accurately rendered folding chair, humorously suggesting, perhaps, a Pietà.

In spite of its uncanny "realism" and humor, *9 Objects* was not admired critically when it was first exhibited, owing largely to Richter's insistence on cheapening the production values of his print projects in order to avoid the pratfalls or slickness of Photo-Realism. In retrospect his daring use of photography appears radical, and his insouciant use of commercial printing methods (like that of his German peers, such as Sigmar Polke [see p. 50]) continues to be a powerful influence on younger artists today. **M. P.**

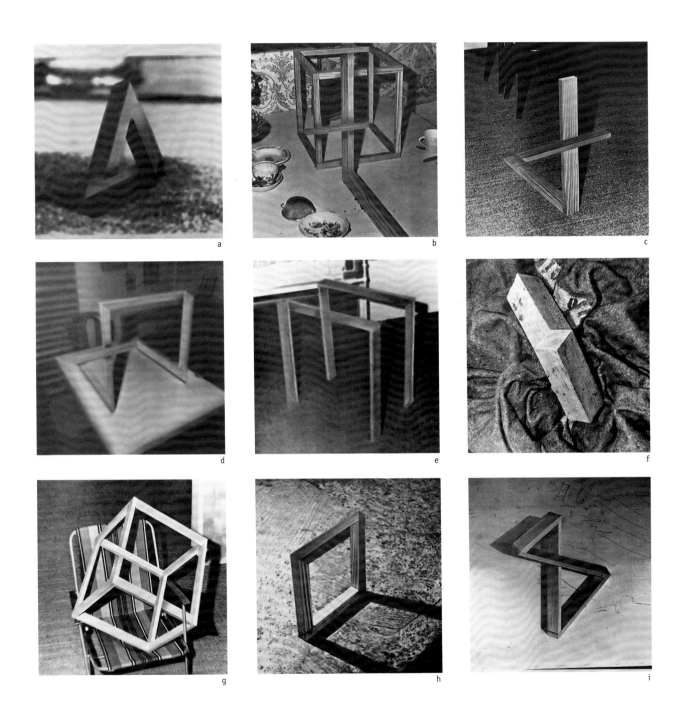

Second Poem Piece, 1969

Inscribed and stamped steel; 152.3 x 152.4 x 1.3 cm (60 x 60 x ½ in.) [see p. 92]

I n the mid-1960s, Bruce Nauman abandoned traditional painting and sculpture and began a self-conscious and critical examination of the role of language in visual art. Since then experiments with wordplay, puns, and jokes have formed a crucial component of his artistic vocabulary. Indeed, Nauman at times privileges the linguistic content of his practice over its visual aspects. Early in his career, the artist was profoundly influenced by the writings of the French novelist and critic Alain Robbe-Grillet and the British playwright Samuel Beckett, two authors notable for their use of repetition, irony, paradox, and unexpected word changes. Additionally, the theoretical musings of the German philosopher Ludwig Wittgenstein—particularly his *Tractatus Logico-Philosophicus* (1922) and *Philosophical Investigations* (*Philosophische Untersuchungen*; 1953)— introduced Nauman to the notion that language can be considered, in terms of visual-art practice, simply as a set of propositions that image the world.[1]

Often, Nauman's literary gymnastics can be found in his titles. In a pencil study from 1966 called *Love Me Tender, Move Te Lender* (Saint Louis Art Museum), for example, Nauman displayed the process of transforming Elvis Presley's popular ballad from sappy love song to confusing riddle. At other times, however, his use of direct-address language incorporates a performative aspect, inviting viewers to experience the logic (or illogic) of the text by reading or speaking it themselves. In later works such as the neon signs *Raw War* (1970), *Run From Fear, Fun From Rear* (1972), and *One Hundred Live and Die* (1984), Nauman extended his interest in simple wordplay to the highest levels of his ambition and achievement.

Preceding his mature work in neon, Nauman's interest in linguistic gamesmanship can be traced back to two somewhat exceptional flat, steel wall sculptures with inscribed text executed in 1968 and 1969. In his *First Poem Piece* (1968; Otterlo, Rijksmuseum Kröller-Müller), he inscribed the words YOU, MAY, NOT, WANT, TO, BE, HERE (HEAR) in vertical columns. In *Second Poem Piece*, he similarly positioned the words YOU, MAY, NOT, WANT, TO, SCREW, HERE (or HEAR) across the sculpture's surface. In both of the poem pieces, the progressive removal of one or more words from the original sentence produces different sentences in each horizontal row. Although all of the sentences are complete, they do not construct a conventional narrative. "What I was interested in was that art generally adds information to a situation," Nauman has stated, "and it seems reasonable to also be able to remove information from a situation and get art from that."[2] The eighteen possible variations in *Second Poem Piece* include "You may not want to screw here," "You may want to screw here," "You want to screw," "You may not hear," "You may not want to hear," and finally, "You want." The word "screw" in particular invites a host of witty vernacular associations, ranging from the banal (manual labor at a construction site) to the provocative (sexual intercourse).

As is often the case with Nauman's work, there is a tension between the form and the content of *Second Poem Piece*. By the late 1960s, the reductive, industrial forms of Minimalist sculpture—pioneered by Judd, LeWitt, Morris, Serra, and others—had come to the forefront of the contemporary art scene. At the same time, however, Conceptual artists such as Lawrence Weiner and Joseph Kosuth were beginning their groundbreaking explorations of language as a sculptural form in and of itself. Rejecting the rigid structuralism of academic Minimalism, Nauman employed his trademark humor to subvert an otherwise purely formal sculptural idiom. Here, the permanence of inscribed steel is at odds with the ever-evolving nature of its language-based meaning.

The result is a sly parody of what the artist perceived to be the high-minded seriousness of much Minimalist sculpture. Whether in drawing, sculpture, or neon, Nauman always insists on language's inability to deliver a fixed or stable set of meanings. In his own desire to keep the viewer off guard, he calls attention to the deceptive potential in all sign systems. **J. E. R.**

Studies for Holograms, 1970

Five screenprinted duotones on paper; each 66 x 66 cm (26 x 26 in.) [see pp. 92–93]

From 1965 to the present, Bruce Nauman has worked concurrently in several media. In addition to the sculpture for which he is best known, Nauman has made films, video installations, and photographs, as well as numerous drawings and prints. In his pluralistic approach, he epitomizes the model for post-World War II artistic practice. Like Gerhard Richter (see p. 36), Nauman used photography early on in his career, in 1966 creating color photographs that were daring at the time for their artless and perfunctory nature.[1] The artist's motivations for producing such photographs may be likened to Richter's decision to paint from photographs beginning in 1962. Both chose to work with photography in part because it could be identified with non-art functions.[2] Specifically, Nauman and Richter deliberately worked in opposition to the prevailing "fine-print" aesthetic—exemplified by the lithographs of Jasper Johns and the products of well-known workshops of that time—using cheap papers and unseductive mechanical reproduction.[3]

During this early phase in his career, Nauman often employed his own body as a material on which and with which to act. *Studies for Holograms* for example depicts the artist's face, distorted in various ways. As he put it:

The idea of making faces had to do with thinking of the body as something you can manipulate. I had done some performance pieces—vigorous pieces dealing with standing, leaning, bending—and as they were performed, some of them seemed to carry a large emotional impact.[4]

This portfolio, Nauman's first print project, refers to work he had created in other media during the immediate past: a series of films made in 1968–69,[5] the group of holograms collectively known as *First Hologram Series: Making Faces* (a–k) of 1968, and a drawing (fig. 1). That the artist explored this theme in such a broad range of media underscores its importance within his oeuvre. Nauman has stated that he felt he did not possess the necessary skill to create these images as paintings. Ultimately, he chose photography and photo-imaging methods because he found them to be the most direct way to produce the work.

The five prints are screenprinted duotones, photomechanically reproduced from infrared photographs that were taken in preparation for Nauman's first holograms.[6] While the holograms depict the artist's full face, the prints are cropped below the eyes, focusing our attention on the lips and neck, and their distortion by his movements. These— pinched and pulled lips (a, b, e), pinched cheeks (c), and pulled neck (d)—appear playful and banal, exactly like what a bored child might do to amuse himself. However, the larger-than-life scale of the images, the nauseatingly yellow coloration, and the cheap, commercial aspect of the printing and paper combine to produce a disturbing effect.

While it has been noted that Nauman's prints have an affinity with the self-portrait sculpture of the mentally disturbed Viennese artist Franz Xaver Messerschmidt (1736–1783), Nauman's expressions are far more mundane.[7] Whereas Messerschmidt portrayed himself grimacing—an act fraught with psychological innuendo—Nauman made faces that exemplify childish insolence. Instead of representing psychic pain in an obvious way, he chose to incite the viewer with impudence. As Paul Schimmel pointed out, Nauman's intent has been to manipulate his audience, using any means necessary to get us to pay attention to his work; the meaning of the work is what it does to us.[8] Indeed, when these prints were exhibited in 1998 at The Art Institute of Chicago, one visitor asked with disgust whether we "could have chosen a more uninviting, unpleasant welcome into the galleries," to which Nauman might have responded, "EXACTLY!" **M. P.**

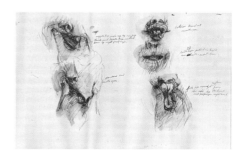

FIGURE 1 Bruce Nauman. *Mouths*, 1967. Pen and black ink and brush and gray wash on paper; 48.2 x 69.2 cm (19 x 27¼ x in.). New York, Joseph Helman Collection.

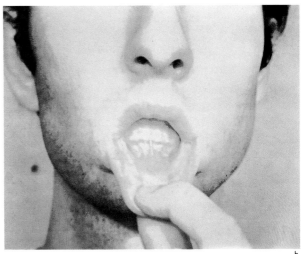

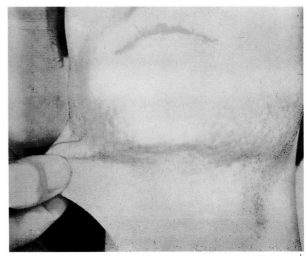

American Costume, 1970

Mixed media on paper; 62.2 x 49.2 cm (24½ x 19⅜ in.) [see p. 90]

This image, which initially appears to be a drawing or a print, is in fact a direct impression of David Hammons's own body. *American Costume* is one of a number of works that Hammons produced from the late 1960s through 1975 using his form as the primary printing template.[1] His technique involved smearing his body, hair, and clothes with a greasy substance, such as butter, and then pressing himself onto a picture surface. Next he dusted the stained surface with chalk or graphite to render the physical impressions more clearly. Here a variety of textured areas, indicating hair, a collar, and a garment, frame the profiled facial features. The artist reproduced his own face in the image by pressing it directly onto the paper; he fashioned the hair and collar out of thumbprints; and used the residual traces of some type of fibrous material, perhaps fur or hair, to represent the garment.

Born in 1943 in Springfield, Illinois, Hammons moved to Los Angeles, where he began his formal artistic training. While a student at the Otis Art Institute, he studied with the noted African American artist Charles White, who had been employed by the federally funded Works Progress Administration in the 1930s.[2] White's socially directed oeuvre had a strong impact on the young artist's perspective: working at a time defined by social strife, political activism, and a focus on civil rights, Hammons conceived of his art as an active response to his milieu.

As the Civil Rights movement gained momentum, white Americans began to acknowledge the diversity of the nation's population and to confront the injustices informing African Americans' daily experiences. Although heightened awareness effected some change, non-white Americans still have had to face inequality, poverty, and, not infrequently, physical harm on a regular basis. *American Costume* engages ethnocentric generalizations related to an expanding definition of what being an American means and whom it includes; it also foregrounds ironies of contemporary social realities. Here Hammons emphasized his African descent by accentuating certain physical characteristics. The vertical striations on the cheek recall similar treatments on bronze portrait busts from the Benin region of West Africa. The distinct facial features and the textures of the hair and dress imbue the image with a marked "otherness"—unfamiliarity, in this case from a Eurocentric perspective—that taps into racial stereotypes deeply embedded in the American consciousness.[3] The title is especially revealing of the artist's intentions: in conjunction with the image, it generates a sense of dissonance and tension. The word "costume" suggests something artificial or masked, as well as the temporary adoption of a non-quotidian or "exotic" identity. The adjective "American," with its mainstream, patriotic overtones, has critical implications, as if Hammons wanted to suggest that white viewers might see this figure as somehow outside their understanding of American-ness.

Hammons became known in the late 1960s for appropriating found objects,[4] most notably refuse, such as scraps of metal and wood, hair cuttings, chicken bones, bottles, dirt, and grease—familiar, available materials, comprising the stuff of daily life. His use of his own body as both subject and object is an extension of this approach. By finding new contexts for such substances—the residue of resources or commodities that have been processed and discarded by a particular social group—Hammons addressed a variety of issues relevant to his own identity as an African American and an artist. Works such as *American Costume* draw attention to the exclusion of blacks from the social privileges enjoyed by most white Americans, and to the same type of exclusion black artists confront in the art world. Rejecting the traditional materials associated with canonical fine art, Hammons facilitated an identification with the art object by black audiences, who can see their own social experiences reflected in his media and subject matter. **R. H. D.**

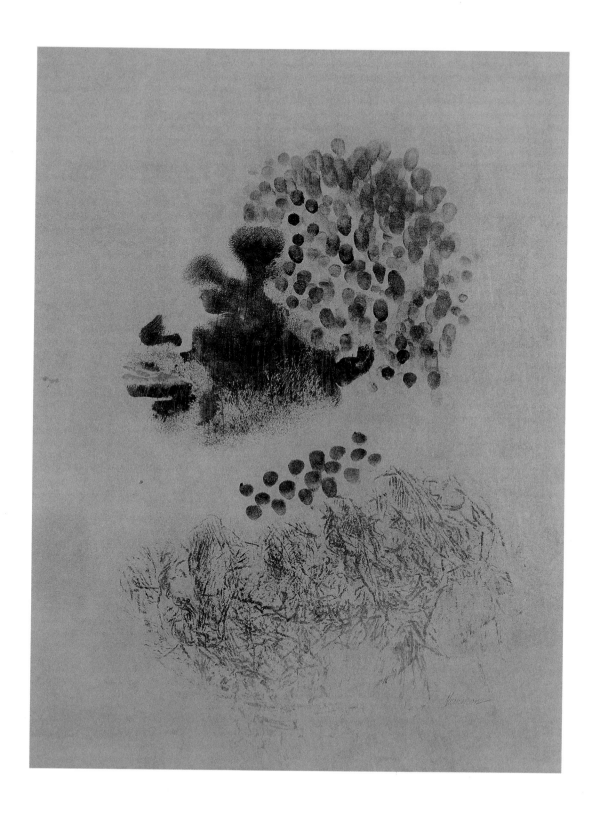

Brice Marden (AMERICAN; BORN 1938)

Rodeo, 1971

Oil and beeswax on two canvases; 243.8 x 243.8 cm (96 x 96 in.) [see p. 91]

During the past four decades, Brice Marden has played a key role in maintaining the vitality of abstract painting. *Rodeo*, a work of imposing scale and stark presence, represents a high point of his early career. Two rectangular canvas panels, one yellow, the other gray, are joined to form an eight-foot square. Each canvas is pulled across a deep (two and one-eighth-inch) stretcher and painted with a medium that combines oil paint and beeswax. The stretcher and thick, opaque pigment give to *Rodeo* a sense of weight and a sculptural presence, qualities complemented by the iconic simplicity of the painting's composition. The oil-and-beeswax surface absorbs light and inhibits reflections; it is remarkably even in tone, material, matter-of-fact. And yet this very materiality and insistence also suggest depth. There seems the possibility that, beneath the impassive surface of *Rodeo*, something lies hidden.

The line joining the two panels may suggest a horizon line, and thus a landscape. The juxtaposition of two rectangular fields also recalls the work of Mark Rothko. However, whereas Rothko's floating, horizontal fields are transparent, shimmering, and evanescent, Marden's twin panels seem determinedly earthbound, presented as physical facts rather than as expressions of spiritual aspiration. Still, something of the mystery so powerfully expressed in Rothko's work is also present in *Rodeo*. This results partly from Marden's colors, rendered vaguely unfamiliar by the paint-and-wax medium. The word "yellow" for example hardly captures the color or tone of the top panel of *Rodeo*, even though no other word, or combination of words, can easily describe it. Moreover, the medium affects the relation between the two colors: the yellow and gray panels, which we would expect to advance and recede, remain uncannily suspended on the same plane.

Marden's paintings of the 1960s and 1970s, with their joined monochrome panels, repeated shapes, and hard-edged colors, are often linked to the tenets of Minimalism. However, Marden's practice cannot be adequately contained by the painter Frank Stella's famous dictum, "What you see is what you see." Like all of Marden's paintings, *Rodeo* is handmade. Its composition, two equal panels that form a square, reveals a clear and rational a priori structure, while its surface is the product of an unusually laborious process. Keeping his paint-and-wax mixture warm in a pot on the stove, Marden laid layer upon layer of the medium over his canvas panels to achieve a virtually uniform surface. Because it is largely unaccented, that surface displays little of the process of its making. Neither, however, does it suggest pure logic nor does it offer a moment of unmediated perception. *Rodeo* is among the most bold and striking of Marden's paintings; it is also subtle and mysterious. The work's even, dully glowing yellow and gray surfaces, the apparent weight of the painting, and its physicality all suggest that something unseen, but nevertheless felt, operates upon the viewer's perceptions. With *Rodeo* what you see is also what you do not see. **J. S.**

Bronze Chair, designed 1972, cast 1975
Bronze; 121.9 x 45.7 x 50.8 cm (48 x 18 x 20 in.) [see p. 86]

During the course of a relatively short career, Scott Burton created extraordinary works of art that blur the boundaries between sculpture and furniture. Best known for meticulously crafted pieces made of stone, metal, and concrete, Burton consistently demonstrated a profound awareness of aesthetics and utility. As a locus for explorations of both form and function, the chair occupies a position of singular importance within the context of Burton's larger oeuvre.

Bronze Chair is the artist's first studio object. It was cast from an actual wooden dining-room chair that Burton found in 1970 among the items left behind by the previous tenant of his apartment in lower Manhattan. Burton described the chair—a relatively inexpensive, contemporary reproduction of a nineteenth-century English design—as "Grand Rapids Queen Anne."[1] The comment brilliantly evokes the evolution of the chair's identity from the highbrow associations of an original period piece to the distinctly middle-class realm of the contemporary massproduced imitation. Burton recognized the irony, even the poetry, in this solitary, discarded, visibly used chair (the slightly bent frame indicates that it had been "broken in" by its previous owner). He immediately incorporated the chair into his "tableaux" works (1970–71), a series of performance-based, temporary installations and static arrangements of found and altered pieces of furniture. In 1972 the artist decided to cast the chair in bronze. As an exercise, he first painted the original wood frame with metallic paint. The actual casting took place in 1975.[2]

This piece perhaps illustrates better than any other the essential processes of translation that were at the heart of Burton's lifelong project. In material terms, the casting transformed the "cast-off" chair from a humble, decorative-art object into a precious, fine-art object. Although *Bronze Chair* was conceived as a studio piece for gallery presentation, the casting also relocated the chair from the context of domestic space into the language of public sculpture. In typical Burton fashion, he exhibited the work for the first time on the sidewalk outside of Artists Space, an alternative arts organization in New York City, in 1975 (see fig. 1). This initial exhibition of *Bronze Chair* inverted established

notions of private and public use. Throughout his career, Burton chose to make both studio objects for traditional gallery presentation and site-specific projects for public spaces. It is in the latter context that Burton is perhaps best understood. Above all else, he wanted to engage social space, and he often expedited the process by placing his pieces outdoors.[3] All of Burton's works, regardless of placement, carry the potential for practical public use.

Burton's early studio pieces, from *Bronze Chair* until the end of the 1970s, began as found objects. Thus, they acquired meaning in relation to existing associations with popular vernacular design. In the 1980s, Burton moved decisively into the realm of original design, producing rigorously reductive, geometric, and abstract works. *Aluminum Chair* of 1980–81 (Checklist no. 6) and *Low Piece (Bench)* of 1985–86 (Checklist no. 7), both of which were acquired by the Art Institute through the gift of Lannan Foundation,[4] are typical examples of the artist's mature style. All three attest to Burton's passion for colliding fine art and practical design, and, in the process, opening up the scope of inquiry for both disciplines. J. E. R.

FIGURE 1 Scott Burton. *Bronze Chair*, exhibited outside Artists Space, New York, 1975.

Lucas Samaras (AMERICAN; BORN GREECE, 1936)

Phototransformation (10/25/73), 1973; Phototransformation (4/4/76), 1976; Phototransformation (7/31/76), 1976

Internal dye-diffusion transfer prints (Polaroids); each 7.6 x 7.6 cm (3 x 3 in.) [see p. 96]

These three photographs represent early experiments by Lucas Samaras with a nascent Polaroid technology. The images are self-portraits, in which Samaras captured himself in a variety of poses. The photographs are jewel-like in their intimate scale, rich color, and reflective, sometimes textured, surfaces. Although the artist became interested in Polaroid photography in 1969, he did not explore it until 1973, when he and a number of other artists each received the newly invented SX-70 camera from an employee of the Polaroid Corporation, John Holmes. Holmes asked the artists to experiment with the new device and produce photographs for an exhibition to be held at the Light Gallery, New York. Subsequently, from 1973 to 1976, Samaras generated a series of Polaroid images that expanded the representational boundaries of photography by manipulating the actual substance of the medium itself.

The Polaroid technology Samaras employed utilized film that consisted of a semiliquid, chemical emulsion encased within two plastic layers.[1] When an object was shot, the image became imprinted in the emulsion and gradually developed as the chemicals processed. The Polaroid reproduction could be substantially altered by physically rearranging the soft emulsion, but changes to the pictorial format had to be made within a limited time period—less than a minute—because, after the emulsion solidified and the image completely resolved, its substance could no longer be manipulated. Exploring this process, Samaras photographed himself in staged settings in his New York apartment. He then applied a pointed tool to the surface of the Polaroid shell to shift the emulsion within its casing, distorting the photographed shapes as they developed.

The Polaroids allowed Samaras to explore ideas he had first investigated in pastel drawings from 1957 to 1965 (see fig. 1). Although the photographs and the pastels differ in terms of medium and technique, they are conceptually and formally linked. The drawings, depicting portraitlike faces in various stages of metamorphosis and states of being, foreshadowed the photographs' protean figures. Both kinds of works exhibit two modes of figural representation: one, an undefined figure in a state of total corporeal flux; and two, a body retaining some measure of its physical integrity, yet demonstrating a distortion, displacement, or substitution of its constituent elements. The ambiguous faces seen in the pastels, however, possess no relationship to the appearance of an actual body. Composed of layers of powdered pigments on the picture surface, the rendered forms are completely imaginary and can thus be viewed as visual expressions of memory and feeling, and as purely formal concoctions. The Polaroid, on the other hand, provided a pre-set matrix whose subject, although later altered, was initially captured from life through a mechanical process. The fantastic forms, the theatrical quality of the exaggerated gestures, and the rapid, almost intuitive, manner in which Samaras manually transformed the Polaroid images not only quote the earlier pastel works but demonstrate Samaras's effective integration of a graphic medium with that of photography. **R. H. D.**

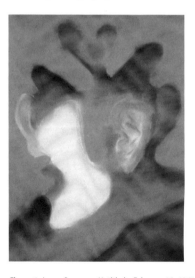

Figure 1 Lucas Samaras. *Untitled—February 16, 1961*, 1961.
Pastel on paper; 30.7 x 22.8 cm (12 1/16 x 8 15/16 in.) [see p. 96].

Uri Geller Welcomes Unknown Beings from the Realm of Fables
(Uri Geller empfängt fremde Wesen aus der Fabel), 1976

Three-part collage with mixed media; prints each 29.2 x 41.9 cm (11½ x 16½ in.) [see p. 93]

The three photo-collages known as *Uri Geller Welcomes Unknown Beings from the Realm of Fables* are part of a thirty-year investigation by Sigmar Polke of "unknown beings" (*fremde Wesen*) and paranormal phenomena. In the late 1960s, Polke devoted a painting, installation, and photographic series to the theme of being directed in his art making by higher life forces, as if he were a conduit through which such forces created his art. Over the next decade, he produced several works about UFOs and psychedelic, extrasensory experiences. The Art Institute of Chicago's photographic essay on Uri Geller—a self-proclaimed telepathic and telekinetic Israeli who in 1972 claimed to have stopped a cable car in mid-air using the power of his mind and, just a few years later, was exposed as a fraud—continues the artist's exploration of the unusual, immaterial, and even alchemical.

For Polke the subject of these photo-collages and the way he made them were interconnected. Drawing upon the supernatural, invisible powers claimed by Geller, the artist unleashed the unknown in the photographic development process. He acted as a medium for the hand of chance by deliberately overlaying and obscuring images in negatives and by ignoring the rules of developing to permit surprise effects. He described this method in 1976, stating, "What appears to be something I have conceived has actually felt its way inside me."[1]

By allowing the unexpected combination of images, as well as their enlargement, Polke summoned new, even grotesque, apparitions on the photographic paper. He employed colored pens and paint to conjure profiles, silhouettes, and diagrams from the jumbled forms. While his use of commercial printing patterns in the *Uri Geller* series reveals his roots in Pop Art aesthetics, the dot pattern here becomes not only an independent formal element but also signals metaphorically an energy field or atmosphere of paranormal activities.

Each photo-collage in the *Uri Geller* series alludes to aspects of telepathy. For example, in the first collage, Polke pasted a commercial illustration of two bears—one dreaming of cost-effective warmth—hibernating in a blizzardlike pattern of enlarged dots. In a figurative sense, the work seems to suggest the inner world of dreams, the realm of the unbridled

subconscious. In the second collage, the printing patterns that form enlarged images combine to produce other images. Polke drew over the dot pattern with orange, purple, and black lines, eliciting figures out of the thicket of points. The chemical murkiness on the upper left and burnt corner in the lower right suggest the use of fire in the practice of magic. Full-frontal and profiled faces populate the second and third collages. In the second work, Polke emphasized the eyes of these minimally indicated visages, as if to suggest the power they have to communicate mentally. The artist incorporated into the final collage a photograph and a cartoon from newspapers to identify the object of the profiled figure's focus (a man shaving) and the humorous outcome of his mental concentration (a man whose face is covered by a dark splatter). The caption at the bottom of the cartoon, "Ohne Worte" (without words), underscores the nonverbal and psychological nature of these interactions.

Technically sophisticated and humorous, *Uri Geller Welcomes Unknown Beings from the Realm of Fables* not only represents a summation of Polke's interests over the ten years that preceded it, but also relates to his present work, in which he overlays enlarged photographic images of printing errors that, isolated as subjects themselves, suggest the mysterious and alchemical elements of art production. **S. D.**

Red Peanut, 1980

Acrylic on cast plaster; 38.4 x 44.1 x 10.8 cm (15⅛ x 17⅜ x 4¼ in.) [see p. 86]

Since the late 1970s, John Ahearn has produced intensely detailed and highly emotive figurative sculpture that portrays the members of the community in which he lives. The artist's process and subjects serve to integrate his art into a social context: he finds his sitters and fabricates his sculpture, using unrefined materials, on the sidewalks of his South Bronx neighborhood. In his work, Ahearn demonstrates and celebrates the possibilities of making a participatory art on the street, outside of established artworld institutions.

In 1977 Ahearn formed Collaborative Projects, Inc. (Colab), with a group of fellow artists, including Jenny Holzer and Kiki Smith (see p. 64). Their aim was to provide a cooperative union for young, unestablished artists who shared a concern for social and political issues. With the intention of challenging existing art systems, Colab staged several controversial and informal exhibitions at alternative spaces, such as the legendary "Times Square Show," held in June 1980. This event—which included sculpture by Ahearn and work by Jean Michel Basquiat and Keith Haring—drew the attention of dealers, collectors, and curators to a new kind of street art. Raw and unpolished in appearance and in theme, this type of work was to have a profound impact on the art trends of the 1980s and 1990s.

Ahearn moved to the South Bronx in 1979 and began to exhibit his art at Fashion Moda, an alternative, artist-run gallery.[1] That same year, he made his first casts from life, using as his subjects his neighbors, predominantly African Americans and Puerto Ricans. Rigoberto Torres, a local resident without formal art training, helped Ahearn develop his casting technique and has collaborated with him for many years. Since the process is labor- and time-intensive, and therefore demanding of the sitter, Ahearn only makes casts of individuals who approach him and volunteer to pose for him. *Red Peanut* depicts a joyous, exuberant young woman from the South Bronx nicknamed "Peanut."[2] Each of Ahearn's sitters becomes a collaborator, as he or she must remain still for hours during the casting process. Ahearn begins by layering pieces of cloth soaked in wet plaster on the subject's face and body to create a mold. He typically does this outside, on the sidewalk, in order to keep the activity of art making public and to create a community dialogue about the art. Ahearn then executes and paints plaster editions of three. He presents one cast to the sitter, gives another to his dealer for sale, and keeps the third for his own collection. He prefers to exhibit his sculpted portraits on the sides of neighborhood buildings, transforming the recognizable faces of the community into shrine-like architectural adornments.

Ahearn's methods put him in intimate physical and emotional contact with his subjects, and the inherent trust that bonds him to them is demonstrated in the finished sculptures. The narrative and expressive qualities of these works provide an insight into the individuals whom they portray, and also into the inspirational relationship that exists between Ahearn and the members of his community. Through the dignified and respectful representation of his sitters, Ahearn elevates the residents of an urban neighborhood to a monumental, heroic status. S.S.

Thomas Ruff (GERMAN; BORN 1958)

Untitled (Ralph Müller), 1986; Untitled,1988; Untitled, 1988

Chromogenic color prints; 205.1 x 163.2 cm (80¾ x 63¼ in.), 210.8 x 165.1 cm (83 x 65 in.),
210.2 x 165.4 cm (82¾ x 65⅛ in.) [see p. 95]

That Lannan Foundation chose to give the Art Institute all three of the portraits by Thomas Ruff in its collection, instead of dispersing them to three different museums, reflects an insight into the work itself. Although Ruff prints his photographs big enough to force a comparison with contemporary paintings, he also speaks of them as "passport photos" or "mug shots."[1] To get this sense of them—as common, mass-produced images—you must see more than one at a time.

Much of what Ruff says about his portraits draws attention to their identity-card character. In describing his work to the curator Boris von Brauchitsch, for instance, Ruff stated, "Light(ing) floods the entire space, be it in the office, the supermarket, the town square or the underground garage. In other words, everyone is able at all times to make out clearly the other person's well-lit face (and this is, of course, only too useful for closed-circuit TV surveillance). We live in the cities of mass or industrial society, and we are not desperate or sad, yet we nevertheless have nothing to laugh about either."[2] Ruff's words give a human poignancy to his subjects while, at the same time, emphasizing the bureaucratic neutrality of their poses.

Ruff intentionally disassociates himself from the celebration of sensibility to which earlier photographic portraiture sometimes aspired. Brauchitsch was quite right when he observed that "Ruff . . . finds the idea of using photographic means to create a personality abhorrent. He seeks to prove with his portraits that a picture can . . . never reveal the inner truth about a person."[3] Like the mug shot or surveillance videotape, Ruff's portraits quantify their subjects: "the person has been 'thingified,'" as Stephan Dillemuth put it in an interview with Ruff.[4] When we see even three of Ruff's portraits ganged together, their overwhelming similarity makes it clear that they are about an entire generation, not the idiosyncrasies of the individual.

Ruff's is not a very cheerful view of the age in which we live. Had the portraits left us any doubt about this, some of his other series—particularly his late 1980s studies of German housing and his photographs from the early 1990s of far galaxies—make it obvious. The light in his work goes from the blinding brightness of the portraits to the overcast flatness of the workers' houses and the near-total dark of deep space.[5] Taken together, the three projects become pictures of emptiness—the emptiness of modern culture, of contemporary man, and of the universe itself.

Ruff's explicators, including himself, sometimes speak in perplexing tautologies and contradictions. "Are your portraits so obviously portraits precisely because they aren't portraits?" Dillemuth asked Ruff at one point.[6] Explaining to Brauchitsch why he used his friends from the Düsseldorf Akademie as his subjects, Ruff said, "The people have to know what my portraits are like in order to behave in such a way that the result is like one of my portraits."[7] The circularity of such statements about Ruff's art reflects the repetitious nature of the work itself. This is a quality to which it seems condemned by history.

In the Dillemuth interview, Ruff described his work as "imitation" and himself as an "imitator."[8] Coming after the many modernist masters of portraiture, Ruff is a postmodernist. He is part of a generation which feels that in our image-laden, art-conscious culture, repetition is the only significant aesthetic gesture left. For all the glamor and international success that post-modernism has attracted, there has always been a certain dourness about it, a joylessness and self-alienation of the artist from art. This too Ruff's work exemplifies. **C. W.**

Alfredo Jaar (CHILEAN; BORN 1956)

1 + 1 + 1, 1987

Mixed media; 127 x 487.7 x 182.9 cm (50 x 192 x 72 in.) [see p. 91]

Alfredo Jaar's photographic installations address the distance between reality and the representation of reality. Specifically, Jaar explores the ways in which social and economic inequities in the developing world are seen and understood in the industrialized West. Rejecting the opposition of "first" and "third" worlds—and all of the clichéd and pernicious generalizations attached to such classifications—his work exposes the often invisible prejudices embedded in images of cultural difference. Since first coming to prominence in the early 1980s, Jaar has simultaneously asserted and questioned art's ability to raise awareness, solicit empathic response, and effectively advance social justice.

Commissioned for "Documenta 8," held in Kassel, Germany, in 1987, *1 + 1 + 1* responds to the context of this major international exhibition, long dominated by a European perspective. With his work, Jaar was interested in subverting not only "first-world" assumptions about the "third world," but also stereotypical art-world representations of economically and culturally marginalized positions. *1 + 1 + 1* equates the aestheticization of poverty with exploitation. The installation includes one of Jaar's first mature uses of the photographic light box—a glass and metal structure supporting a photographic transparency back-lit by fluorescent tubes—which has become his signature method of presentation. Here, three light boxes are mounted low on the wall; each contains a single black-and-white image of impoverished children standing in a dusty landscape. The photographs are cropped dramatically and presented upside down. While the faces of the children are absent, their bare feet, distended bellies, and partially clothed bodies unmistakably signal the depressed social and economic circumstances in which they live. Three gilded "fine-art" frames—uniformly sized to fit the three light boxes—are positioned on the floor directly in front of the photographs. The left frame is empty, the center frame contains a series of four progressively smaller frames, and the right frame surrounds a mirror.

1 + 1 + 1 challenges the conventional politics of museum or gallery display. Initially, the piece is striking simply because the three photographs are presented upside down. This inversion, however, functions on the level of metaphor as well: the "art" is on the floor (where the viewer stands), and "reality" is on the wall (where the art is hung). The three arrangements of the gilded frame—used here as the iconic representation of an aesthetic experience—offer the art audience three possible ways of looking at "reality." In the first instance, the empty frame speaks to a kind of art entirely divorced from the exigencies of the everyday world. In the center, art appears entirely self-referential, an "art-for-art's-sake" approach that is inconsistent with political or social consciousness. Finally, the framed mirror reflects, and thereby "corrects," the appearance of the photograph. As such it seems to hold out the potential for art to play a useful role in effecting positive change.

Jaar, however, is ultimately pessimistic and deeply conflicted about the potential for art to effect social change. In *1 + 1 + 1*, the mirror is still quite literally circumscribed by the conventions of aesthetic practice. The art object is positioned simply as a passive reflection of prevailing social conditions. The artist's ability to shape a new vision or to alter reality is, by implication, precluded. Not surprisingly, his title makes no evaluative distinction between the three potential strategies. *1 + 1 + 1* suggests, in its inconclusiveness, Jaar's ambivalence about art's ability to directly effect the world's most pressing economic and social problems. **J. E. R.**

Edward Ruscha (AMERICAN; BORN 1937)

F House, 1987
Acrylic on canvas; 116.8 x 203.2 cm (46 x 80 in.) [see p. 96]

Born in Omaha, Nebraska, Edward Ruscha moved to Los Angeles in 1956. Ruscha has explained that he was drawn to the freedom enjoyed by artists working in this "ultimate cardboard cutout town," and fascinated by stereotypical associations of southern California: flexing biceps, suntanned bodies, sunsets, palm trees, cars, superficiality, and the like.[1] Much of his work relates to this setting and the blatant artifice it has come to represent.

From his earliest experiences as a sign painter, Ruscha retained an interest in the visual and conceptual tensions between text and image. He became known in the 1970s for drawings of words set in panoramic landscapes that he executed with technical sophistication. By juxtaposing beautifully rendered lettering and contrived vistas of southern California, Rusha challenged the boundaries between commercial imagery and fine art.

In the late 1980s, Ruscha began to spray acrylic paint onto the canvas with an airbrush—a technique that marks a major departure from his earlier, more traditional methods. Although he previously considered the airbrush too mechanical, he liked the powdery effect—similar to that in dry-pigment drawings (see Checklist no. 65)—it enabled him to produce.[2] One of Ruscha's first works using the airbrush depicts the shadowy figure of an elephant lumbering up an incline (1986; collection of the artist); he subsequently produced a succession of paintings featuring silhouettes of howling coyotes, wagon trains on hills, and ships pitched by a rough sea. While these subjects—somewhat humorous and cartoonish, but with an ironic or ominous edge—were new for Ruscha, they share with the artist's earlier panoramas such elements as diagonally oriented compositions and strong contrasts of lights and darks. Central to the impact of all of these airbrushed works is a murky, nocturnal glow that can seem both comforting and threatening.

In *F House*, Ruscha exploited this double edge in particularly complex and compelling ways. The painting shows a view of a suburban house at night, nestled between silhouettes of trees and bushes. The lights shining through each of the windows, the manicured lawn, and the landscaping suggest that the property is occupied and well-tended. Ultimately, however, none of this protects the dwelling from the sense of danger that seems to haunt it. The block-style letter "F" that floats in front of the house may allude to the F-stop on a camera (photographers use F-numbers to measure the ability of the camera lens to gather light and determine depth of field). The red color of the "F" and its sharp, crisp edges contrast with the black silhouette of the house and grounds, whose blurred outlines suggest an image that is out-of-focus.

On one level, *F House* can be seen as an exploration of the relationship between painting and photography, a long-held interest of the artist. Here, however, Ruscha seems to have been intent on something more: The superimposition of a red motif over the house implies surveillance, by means of a camera, a telescopic lens, or perhaps even the scope of a gun. Suggesting intrusive examination and potential harm, the image evokes many a scene from Hollywood suspense thrillers. In this way, Ruscha invested a benign image of middle-class, suburban prosperity with unsettling and perhaps malevolent overtones. **A. D. B.**

Bruce Nauman (AMERICAN; BORN 1941)

Clown Torture, 1987

Color video, color-video projection, sound; dimensions variable [see p. 93]

Bruce Nauman's wildly influential, relentlessly imitated work explores the poetics of confusion, anxiety, boredom, entrapment, and failure. Although Nauman is a prolific artist who has worked in a wide range of media, video has played a pivotal role in his artistic development. Many of his most important early works grew out of his involvement with experimental film and video in the 1960s. After 1973, however, these media became conspicuously absent from his work. Nauman returned to video in 1985 with renewed enthusiasm. *Clown Torture*, one of the artist's most spectacular achievements to date, marked a major new direction and prefigured his recent, more complex environments involving monitors, projections, and other sculptural elements.

Clown Torture is installed in an enclosed, darkened space. The piece consists of two rectangular pedestals, each supporting two pairs of stacked color monitors (one turned upside down, one turned on its side); two large, color-video projections on two facing walls; and sound from all six video displays. The monitors play four narrative sequences in perpetual loops, each chronicling an absurd misadventure of a clown (played to brilliant effect by the actor Walter Stevens). According to the artist, distinctions may be made among the clown protagonists: one is the "Emmett Kelly dumb clown; one is the old French Baroque clown; one is a sort of traditional polka-dot, red-haired, oversized-shoe clown; and one is a jester."[1] In "No, No, No, No (Walter)," the clown incessantly screams the word "no" while jumping, kicking, or lying down; in "Clown with Goldfish," the clown struggles to balance a fish bowl on the ceiling with the handle of a broom; in "Clown with Water Bucket," the clown repeatedly opens a door booby-trapped with a bucket of water that falls on his head; and finally, in "Pete and Repeat," the clown succumbs to the terror of a seemingly inescapable nursery rhyme ("Pete and Repeat are sitting on a fence. Pete falls off. Who's left? Repeat . . . ").

A changing selection of one of the four clown performances is projected on the wall adjacent and to the right of the monitors. The rotation is constant, producing occasional overlaps with the monitor-based presentation of the same sequence. The opposite wall is reserved for a single sequence Nauman called "Clown Taking a Shit," in which the off-duty entertainer is recorded by a security surveillance camera while using a public bathroom. The presentation of the five sequences in six locations is simultaneous, and the relentless repetition produces an almost painful sensory overload for the viewer. With both clown and viewer locked in an endless loop of failure and degradation, the humor soon turns to horror.

Nauman's entire oeuvre can be read as a self-conscious investigation into the conditions and possibilities of art making itself. In his early work, the artist often used his own body as the vehicle for these explorations (see pp. 40–41). Around 1970, however, Nauman himself disappeared from the work entirely. Since that time, he has used the clown— equal parts funny and creepy—as a stand-in for the artist in a number of pieces.[2] More specifically, the clown parodies the artist's own insecurities about producing art. An intensely private individual, Nauman has long been wary of the ways in which art-world success and critical recognition can ultimately reduce the artist's role to that of a "court jester."[3] With *Clown Torture*, Nauman confronted his fear head-on by making public the painful spectacle of a performer trapped in a terrible logic of his own making. And even during the most private of moments, when the performance is over and polite society deems we should be left to our own devices, Nauman suggests that the invasive surveillance— by an ever more curious market demanding "new tricks"— continues. **J. E. R.**

Kiki Smith (AMERICAN; BORN GERMANY, 1954)

Untitled, 1988

Ink on gampi paper; 121.9 x 96.5 x 17.8 cm (48 x 38 x 7 in.) [see p. 97]

K iki Smith's highly individual figurative sculpture examines the physical and spiritual nature of the human body by presenting it in an abject, fragmented, and damaged state. Smith challenges and contradicts classical representations of the body as an absolute, universal form. Her use of decorative, domestic, and organic materials, such as sheets, glass beads, hair, and thread, further trangresses the hierarchy of artistic media. Often labeled as a feminist artist because she incorporates these materials into her work and frequently chooses female subjects, Smith addresses social and political issues in an intensely personal and intimate manner. Her provocative sculpture conveys the vulnerability of the body in an age when medical and technological advancements encourage a false sense of power and control. Smith has observed: "Our bodies are basically stolen from us, and my work is about trying to reclaim one's own turf, or one's own vehicle for being here, to own it and to use it to look at how we are here."[1]

Smith's career began in the 1980s, when many artists used representations of the body to examine issues of gender politics and identity. Her art is rooted in the Post-Minimalism of the 1960s and 1970s, particularly as practiced by Louise Bourgeois, Eva Hesse, and Nancy Spero, each of whom has worked in expressive and figurative modes, utilizing humble, malleable materials such as latex, cloth, paper, and wax. Smith has also cited late Gothic wooden carvings and early Northern Renaissance altarpieces, with their elongated, hyperextended depictions of Christ, as inspirations for her sculpture. In addition she has been influenced by the figures in Egyptian and Indian art, and by decorative art of all kinds. Medicine, anthropology, and anatomy have further informed her interest in the body, and in 1985 she trained as an emergency medical technician to better understand how the body functions in states of trauma and crisis. At this time, she began making sculpture that explicitly addresses issues of corporeality.[2]

Untitled is one of only a few sculptures executed by Smith that investigates the male form.[3] In this construction, the flayed, bloodied, empty skin of a dismembered masculine head, torso, and limbs hangs limply from the wall. The body, once full of mass and energy, is now deflated and void

of life. Smith used tissue-thin gampi paper—a fragile, ephemeral material—to convey the porous and permeable quality of human skin.

Like much of Smith's work, *Untitled* is at once disturbing and beautiful. The artist's Catholic upbringing shaped her attitudes about physical suffering, failure, and death, and contributed to her fascination with the relationship between bodily systems and emotion, spirituality, and sexuality. The death of Smith's father, the architect and Minimalist sculptor Tony Smith, in 1980, followed by that of her sister, Beatrice, eight years later, had a profound effect on her art. During this period, Smith created *Untitled* and some of her most arresting and visceral sculptural forms. She has stated: "I grew up in a family with lots of illness. There was a preoccupation with the body. Also being Catholic, making things physical, they're obsessed with the body. It seemed to me to be a form that suited me really well—to talk through the body about the way we're here and how we're living."[4] **S. S.**

Eviscerated Corpse, 1989

Found stuffed animals, sewn together; dimensions variable [see p. 91]

Mike Kelley takes pleasure in perversion and embraces bad taste. He first gained recognition in the underground music and performance scene in southern California in the late 1970s. Since 1986 he has received widespread critical acclaim for his sculptural installations made with stuffed animals and dolls that he finds in bargain bins and thrift shops. Used, soiled, and discarded, Kelley's pathetic toy orphans violate the sentimental association of youth with innocence. "Because dolls represent such an idealized notion of childhood," Kelley has said, "when you see a dirty one you think of a fouled child. And so you think of a dysfunctional family."[1] With scathing black humor and the glee of an adolescent prankster, Kelley seems to relish such images of humiliation and degradation. His determined celebration of the abject is at once a whimsical caricature and a disturbing grotesque.

Eviscerated Corpse, one of Kelley's best-known objects, comes from a series he entitled *Half a Man*, an ironic acknowledgment of the unconventional gender politics underlying his seemingly inappropriate desire to play with crafts, sewing, and stuffed animals. Feminized and infantilized, Kelley positions his process as a transgression of masculine tropes of art making. The work takes as its point of departure the head of a small, female doll mounted on the wall at eye level. Her wide eyes, round mouth, and floppy arms suggest a common, if slightly old-fashioned, Kewpie doll. In place of a body, however, Kelley used a ragged assemblage of soft dolls and stuffed animals to fashion an obscenely exaggerated, womblike form extending from below the doll's head to the floor. A serpentine chain of stuffed animals, sewn end to end, spills out of the hollow cavity, suggesting the entrails promised by the title. The strange biomorphic forms spiral across the gallery floor, a dysfunctional daisy chain of stuffed worms and bananas that ends with an oversized snake. Hardly the apotheosis of a sinister phallic fiend, however, Kelley's monster is pink, soft, and fuzzy.

Kelley first became interested in stuffed animals for their role within what he perceives to be a tainted economy of exchange between adults and children. Toys are after all most often purchased by adults and given to children as gifts. For Kelley this transaction of emotional capital represents a manipulative exercise of power and control: adult generosity exacts a psychic debt of obligation from the child. As Howard Fox has written, "in interpreting the transaction of the gift as a subtle kind of indentured servitude, Kelley impeaches the whole idea of giving, even the humblest of gifts."[2]

Kelley has long been obsessed with the body and its various functions, and the strange, cartoonish horror of *Eviscerated Corpse* presents childhood in particular as a kind of pathological condition. Conventional dolls and stuffed animals always lack sexually specific anatomy, a reflection of an adult desire to reinforce and maintain the chastity of children. Kelley has said that "the stuffed animal is a pseudo-child, a cutified sexless being which represents the adult's perfect model of a child—a neutered pet."[3] His vision of childhood, on the other hand, derives from a tumultuous Freudian battleground of competing sexual drives. Indeed, Kelley's icon of childhood is a hypersexualized monster. The tiny doll is either spilling her intestines or giving birth (or both), a horrible conflation of childhood, motherhood, and death. J. E. R.

Ice 1–4 (Eis 1–4), 1989

Four oil paintings on canvas; each 203.2 x 162.6 cm (80 x 64 in.) [see p. 94]

In recent years, some of the most significant achievements in abstract and figurative painting can be claimed by a single artist: Gerhard Richter. Richter has worked in both modes, often simultaneously, over much of his career. Underlying this apparent dichotomy in the artist's practice, however, is a more fundamental unity: all of his work examines the impulses and contradictions of representation.

Richter executed his four *Ice* paintings at a crucial time, in the months following the completion of his most ambitious and controversial Photo Paintings, the series *18 October 1977* (1988; Frankfurt am Main, Museum für moderne Kunst). That fifteen-panel series addressed an event that had shocked Germany and inaugurated a period of national self-doubt: the group suicide, in prison and under suspicious circumstances, of members of the terrorist Red Army Faction, or Baader-Meinhof Gang. The *18 October 1977* series—Richter's first paintings to address an overtly political theme—represented both a departure and a summation for the artist. He imbued these images, ranging from individual gang members lying dead to their massive funeral, with all the ambiguous, mysterious, and elegiac power his Photo Painting technique could bring to bear.

In the aftermath of *18 October 1977*, Richter turned his attention largely to abstraction. Many of the abstractions of 1988–89 exhibit a dark tonality, with brooding blacks and grays predominating. Dating from the end of this period, the Art Institute's *Ice* paintings exhibit a uniform gray tone that turns silver-frosted, with bits of lively color breaking through their densely layered surfaces. They presage the return to brighter coloration that occurred in Richter's abstractions of 1990. They also show the artist's abstract-painting technique at its most exquisite and refined.

Richter built up each of the four works with multiple layers of paint, laid on with alternating horizontal and vertical strokes, or pulls, of a scraper. Each pull added a film of pigment, but in places may also have dragged up one or more underlying layer. In this way, the history of each painting's making seems simultaneously covered over and revealed.

The artist oriented the top paint layer of *Ice 1* horizontally; this canvas is dominated by icy blue and frosty white tones. In *Ice 2* by contrast a white field of paint, dragged

vertically, predominates. The most colorful of the four *Ice* paintings, *Ice 2* is enlivened by jewel-like bits of yellow, red, and blue that sit above or beneath the white surface. The starkest, darkest of the four paintings, *Ice 3*, features a top layer, pulled horizontally, in which white contrasts with blue-gray and black tones. Finally, *Ice 4* arrests the alternation of horizontal and vertical strokes with a diagonal pull that effectively brings the series to a close. The palette of *Ice 4* is closest to that of *Ice 1*, although the white tones are less assertive and the painting more resolved than *Ice 1*.

The development of Richter's attitude toward abstract painting can be read as moving from a demonstration of the empty and arbitrary nature of abstraction to an acceptance of its capacity to convey meaning. Moved by the complex and contradictory tragedy of the Baader-Meinhof deaths, Richter seemingly gave himself over to the metaphoric rhetoric of painting and to the pictorial language of tragedy. With the *Ice* paintings, that pictorial language is still in place, but to it has been added a metaphoric suggestion of resolution and hope. **J. S.**

Ice 1

Ice 2

Ice 3

Ice 4

Gary Hill (AMERICAN; BORN 1951)

Inasmuch As It Is Always Already Taking Place, 1990

Mixed media; niche: 40.6 x 137.2 x 167.6 cm (16 x 54 x 66 in.) [see p. 91]

L ike most of Gary Hill's video-installation projects, *Inasmuch As It Is Always Already Taking Place* explores the complex relationship between the body and language, or being and knowing. The piece consists of sixteen video monitors positioned within a deep niche. Varying in size from twenty-three inches to one-half inch, the cathode-ray tubes, which have been stripped from their housings, present tightly cropped video images of a male nude at rest: strange, human landscapes comprised only of rib cage, ear, hand, forehead, neck, spine, or mouth, all barely animated by the movement of breathing or swallowing. Two of the smallest monitors (actually eyepieces salvaged from a video camera) show pages of text: in one the pages are being thumbed, and in the other the text is too small to read. Emitted through ten channels are sounds of trickling water, breathing, the clicking of tongue against palate, and a voice whose statements range from the philosophical ("It was only an idea. I couldn't say it any other way") to the practical ("At the level of my mouth. Quick, a glass of water"). These sounds, in combination with the compelling images, tempt the viewer to come as close as physically possible to the piece.

Although Hill brings to his video installations concerns derived from post-modern, deconstructionist literary theory that challenge the perceived unity and purity of modernism, his work operates on a very direct level. The Art Institute's richly textured but disturbing piece alludes to a number of interesting dichotomies: private/public, mind/body, perception/being. Lit harshly, photographed from eccentric angles, and cropped mysteriously, the pictures stretched over the tubes comprise a disassembled body that resists recognition. Hill described the images piled up in the niche as "a kind of debris—bulbs that have washed up from the sea."[1]

Hill's work seems to confront us with the paradoxical manner in which we experience the world from our own bodies, demonstrating that states of seeing, feeling, and naming can contradict one another within the same body. *Inasmuch As It Is Always Already Taking Place* also suggests that our existence is more contingent and provisional than we imagine. Separated from the rest of the world by a sepulchral niche, the artwork also acts as a memento mori, reminding us that life is not only short, but the processes of our knowing it are complicated and perhaps never find resolution. **D. S.**

Alex, 1991

Oil on canvas; 254 x 213.4 cm (100 x 84 in.) [see p. 87]

huck Close does not like to dwell on what he calls "the gimp factor"—the state of quadriplegia in which he was left when an artery in his spine collapsed in December 1988. But it seems impossible to leave this catastrophe out of account when discussing the significance of his 1991 painting *Alex*. "The event" (again Close's term) interrupted his career but did not destroy it. Within a couple of years, he picked up pretty much where he had left off as a painter. The fact that his subject matter never varies—it has always been the human face, tightly framed—calls attention to facture as the aspect of his paintings that subtly changes over time. No works provide a clearer measure of his progress during the period just before and after his paralysis than the series depicting Alex Katz that culminated in the 1991 *Alex*. Considered together, these portraits in various media provide a journal of the plague years in Close's life.

In 1987 Close made twenty-four-by-twenty-inch Polaroids of a group of fellow artists that included Cindy Sherman, Lucas Samaras, and Francesco Clemente as well as Katz. Following his usual practice, Close then turned select Polaroids into maquettes for oil paintings of each of these figures in 1987–88.[1] "I did a color version of Alex [Toledo Museum of Art] for my last show before I went into the hospital," Close recalled during a conversation with Katz published in 1997. "Then the first painting I made in the hospital was [a] small painting of Alex that I made on the first sort of laptop, handicapped-accessible easel devised for me. . . . That was an amazing experience. . . . I painted it with tears dripping down my face."[2]

Thanks to therapy and pure grit, Close had recovered enough use of his arms by 1989 to guide a paintbrush clamped into a brace on his hand. In the painting referred to in the quotation above, a thirty-six-by-thirty-inch portrait entitled *Alex II* (private collection), the handling of the paint is *very* loose. But then Close's brushwork had been getting looser since 1980, when he had begun to paint in oils after giving up the airbrush technique. Like the 1987 *Alex*, done shortly before his "event," the 1989 *Alex II* has incremental blips of paint—circles, dots, and dashes—laid into a grid corresponding to that with which Close had squared off

the Polaroid. In 1990 he painted another *Alex* (private collection) that moved closer to the 1987 version by opening the subject's mouth again (in *Alex II*, he had closed it, as if the conversation between the two artists were suddenly suspended). Finally, in this 1991 work, Close returned to the scale of the 1987 painting—one hundred by eighty-four inches—thereby demonstrating the same control of the paint that he had had before "the event."

Unlike the 1987 and 1989 portraits, those of 1990 and 1991 revert to something closer to the monochrome of the original black-and-white Polaroid.[3] Perhaps this is why the subject seems so grim in the Chicago painting. His brow is knotted over the bridge of his nose, and his parted lips are pulled back over his teeth as if he were in a state somewhere between mental anguish and physical pain. The effect is so profound that, at one point in their 1997 conversation, Close and Katz seemed confused about exactly whose portrait it was. When Katz said he saw in the painting that "you were in a rage," Close asked, "My rage or yours?"[4]

That Close might have been raging against life because of what had happened to him would be understandable. But he was also inspired by the struggle to recover his craft. Of the small, 1989 *Alex II*, Close said, "It really deals with the dichotomy of how depressed I was and, at the same time, how pleased to be back at work."[5] The same mixed emotions are evident, and perhaps finally in the process of resolution, in the *Alex* of 1991. **C. W.**

Alex/Reduction Prints, 1991–93

Fourteen screenprints from a linoleum reduction block on paper; each 182.9 x 147.3 cm (79¾ x 69¼ in.) [see p. 88]

The titles of two articles on Chuck Close in *ARTnews* a few years ago—"Making the Impossible Possible" (May 1992) and "It's Always Nice to Have Resistance" (January 1994)—call attention to Close's love of difficulty. He begins each new project armed only with this love, for he believes that whatever his art is capable of expressing has to be discovered obliquely, by grappling with more concrete and mundane problems of technique, if it is to be discovered at all. Close's career began in earnest in 1967 when he challenged Clement Greenberg's dictum that "the one thing you can't do in art anymore is make a portrait"; that career almost ended in 1988, when a collapsed spinal artery turned Close into a quadriplegic. Having defied Greenberg and then overcome physical catastrophe, Close was ready to try his hand at a linoleum reduction block.

More than merely difficult, this printmaking process is nerve-wracking because a single block is used for all the successive stages through which the image is built up. To further refine the image in the next inking of the block, you have to cut away part of the block's surface as it appeared in the last inking. If you make a mistake, the whole project is ruined. At each point along the way, two impressions are made: a "state proof," which shows that stage of the image in isolation, and a "progressive proof," which shows the accumulated effect of the different states together. As the image disappears in the state proofs, because more and more of the linoleum has been cut away, it gets darker in the progressive proofs, where the ink builds up one layer atop another.

This is a maddeningly paradoxical process. Close says that, with each new alteration of the block, you must focus more on what is being cut away than what is left, since the previous inking is the one that is about to be made irrevocable. In his youth, Close suffered from dyslexia, a condition that he feels affected his visual imagination. It might have come in handy in making these linoleum reduction block prints.

Beyond the difficulties universal to the process, there were others particular to this project. The only press that could handle a block the size that Close wanted was in Madison, Wisconsin. First, Close's flight was canceled due to a winter storm, forcing him to travel to Madison by pickup truck; then the one block of battleship linoleum[1] he had found was shattered in a shipping accident after being left out in the storm. Undeterred, he obtained a sheet of vinyl linoleum as a substitute. His hands were not strong enough to cut vinyl, however, so he hired four cutters to work under his direction. As he wanted to ensure a certain impersonality in the finished work, he also rotated the block at intervals to make the cutters' distinctive marks cancel one another out. Having overcome these problems with the block, Close discovered that the $25,000 batch of Japanese paper took the ink unevenly and stretched on press. His inventive solution was to pull proofs on Mylar that could be transferred directly to silk screen for reproduction later.

The resulting print contrasts sharply with the 1991 painting of the same subject that is its companion piece (see pp. 74–75). Where the painting dissolves Alex Katz's features in a grid of daubs and strokes, the print is hyperdetailed. The painting picks up where Close had left off just before he was paralyzed, while the print seems, as Deborah Wye, a curator at The Museum of Modern Art, New York, observed, "a return to the photographic visual effects of the continuous tone paintings he had done many years before."[2] Like the state proofs and progressive proofs entailed in the reduction process, the final print is both a singular moment that will not recur in Close's career (he says he will not do a reduction print again) and part of the continuum along which that career has progressed from the beginning. **C. W.**

FIGURE 1 Chuck Close. *Alex/Reduction Prints.*

Photo: Ellen Wilson, courtesy Pace-Wildenstein Gallery.

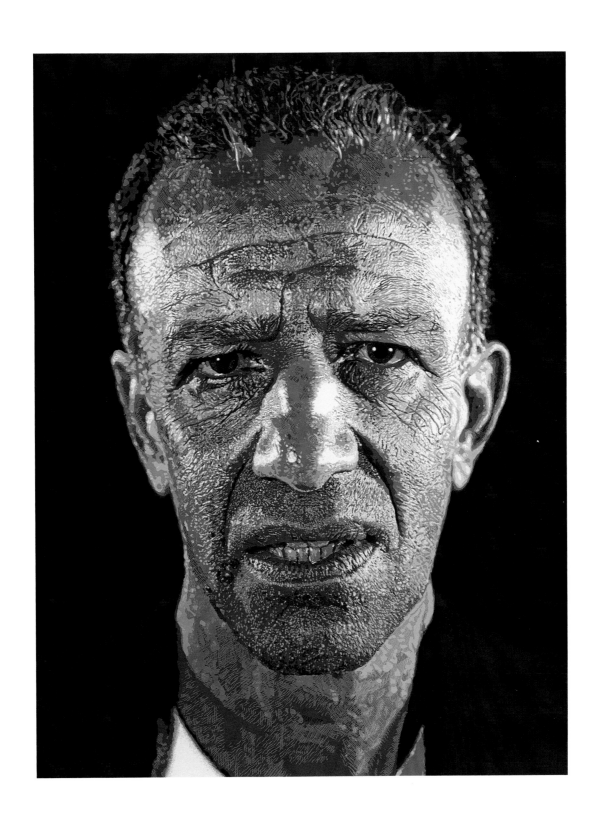

Allen Ruppersberg (AMERICAN; BORN 1944)

Remainders: Novel, Sculpture, Film, 1991

Mixed media; 114.3 x 121.9 x 76.2 cm (45 x 48 x 30 in.) [see p. 95]

The mass-produced book has long been a source of inspiration for Allen Ruppersberg. *Remainders: Novel, Sculpture, Film* is an installation that mimics a publisher's remainders display in a discount bookstore. Hardcover volumes—eight copies of sixteen different novels—are stacked in twenty piles of various heights on a plain wooden table. Ruppersberg borrowed designs for the dust jackets from graphic styles found in his own collection of mid-century movie posters, publicity photographs, greeting cards, calendar art, magazine advertisements, and other such ephemera. As a result, each book has a quaint, slightly out-of-date feel that seems entirely appropriate for the bargain bin. Empty cardboard boxes bearing the imprint of The Vital Line sit on the floor underneath the table. As a sculptural facsimile of a bookstore display, little separates the appearance of Ruppersberg's work from its actual referent in the shopping mall.

Closer inspection, however, reveals that the artist indeed manipulated the presentation in provocative ways. Obviously fictional titles and authors—such as *Pair O' Dice* by I. M. Happier, *Smut* by Mr. Customer, *From Here to Here* by John Doe, Jr., *Ebony, Jade and Ruby (Bad Children)* by J. D., and *The Barriers of Doubt* by George B. George—mingle with the classic *An American Tragedy* by Theodore Dreiser. Perusing the kitschy jokes, catchy wordplays, and corny puns, viewers may well be tempted to browse further. It is then that the transgressive substance of Ruppersberg's installation begins to unfold.

In a museum setting, visitors are seldom able to touch or handle the works of art.[1] Certain aspects of Ruppersberg's project are not readily available to the museum viewer, who has limited access to the books themselves. The back covers and inside jacket flaps of each book for example are printed with the entire screenplay of *LSD–25*, a 1960s educational film that warns of the dangers of hallucinogenic drugs. Inside each book is a series of full-page, black-and-white film stills taken from the artist's archive of over 2,500 industrial and educational films dating from 1931 to 1967, which, if read in sequence, replicate the mechanics of film (twenty-four frames/pages equal one second of film time). The spines of the books feature the names of the films selected, a surreal combination including *A Better Tomorrow*, *Tiny Water Animals*, *Chicken Little Counts to Ten*, and *Atomic Radiation*. The running screenplay and the use of these quirky titles quietly link each of these otherwise disparate objects, incorporating them into a larger narrative of the artist's own making.

Ruppersberg's remaindered books, when placed in a conventional museum installation, function collectively as sculpture instead of literature. They can be seen but not read.[2] As the title of this work indicates, Ruppersberg is interested in translating the literary experience into other media. In 1974 for instance he made a freehand transcription of the entire text of Oscar Wilde's 1891 novel *The Picture of Dorian Gray* on twenty, six-foot-square canvases. Hanging on (and leaning against) the gallery walls, the canvases occupied the position of painting and thus removed any expectation that the novel would be read (at least in its entirety).

That the books in *Remainders: Novel, Sculpture, Film* are not consumed in the typical manner seems to be precisely the point. The "text" of each is absorbed by looking at the objects en masse—the combination of word and image, the period feel of the graphic design, the value judgments associated with multiple unsold copies, and so forth. The cumulative effect of "reading" the books as a sculpture creates an imaginary, free-form text—a new "novel" generated by the interaction between Ruppersberg's creation and the viewer's imagination. Appropriately enough, a quote from the French Symbolist poet Stéphane Mallarmé prefaces each of these literary surrogates: "A book neither begins nor ends. At most, it pretends." **J. E. R.**

Untitled, 1993

String; 90.2 x 81.3 x 81.3 cm (35½ x 32 x 32 in.) [see p. 89]

Tom Friedman operates by training his critical and perceptual faculties on commonplace materials and objects, turning them into something unanticipated and extraordinary. He composed this whimsical piece purely of ordinary cotton string. To achieve this eccentric form, Friedman draped hundreds (perhaps thousands) of lengths of the string upon one another.[1] The result is a three-foot-high sculpture with an unsettling kind of presence. By a process of repetition, the normally lifeless material appears to gather and thrust itself upward, with a slightly tumescent bulge. The cotton fibers on the surface catch the light; the object's silky, gossamer surface suggests both hair and a fountain or waterfall. Friedman has acknowledged an unintended resemblance between his sculpture and "Cousin It," the creature composed purely of hair and eyeglasses from the 1960s television sitcom *The Addams Family*. "It"—the word and the character—is synonymous with the indefinite or ambiguous object.[2]

In his work, Friedman makes art-historical references—both respectful and parodic—that are close to the surface. This untitled string piece shares a strong Dada element with Jean Arp's organic, rising forms; Friedman's draping method—obsessively repeated until it produces a sculptural form of unforeseen proportions and shape—recalls the chance operations of both Arp and Marcel Duchamp. Duchamp himself once used a mile of string in an unprecedented way: to obscure the installation of the historic exhibition "The First Papers of Surrealism," held in New York in 1942. Reflecting more recent trends, *Untitled*'s purity of color brings to mind the Arte Povera works of Piero Manzoni known as "achromes," and Friedman's simple materials and strategy of repetition are related to important aspects of Minimalism and Process Art of the 1960s and 1970s.

But just as Friedman's work engages with major movements of twentieth-century art, it also functions on an intimate level, alluding to how each of us perceives and shapes our individual experience of the world. Friedman has employed such homely materials as chewing gum, pencils, toilet paper, aspirin, laundry detergent, and typing paper—modest, standardized, everyday items that assume an importance disproportionate to their humble origins. The string

piece is one of a series of works addressing the ideas of size, volume, and order. Others include a plastic garbage bag filled to bursting with other garbage bags; a sheet of paper on a pedestal with the exact same dimensions as the paper; and a selection of cheap plastic and rubber balls stolen from stores, entitled *Hot Balls*. String itself has intriguing associative qualities: rarely bought, it is often saved in a kitchen drawer; it appears in fairy tales; and, tied around a finger, it serves as a reminder. For Friedman there is something inherently goofy or "stupid" about this material, something shapeless and trashy.[3] String is, however, useful, and, as Friedman's string piece demonstrates, its applications are ultimately unpredictable. **D. S.**

Gerhard Richter (GERMAN; BORN 1932)

Flowers (Blumen), 1993

Oil on canvas; 72.5 x 102.2 cm (28½ x 40¼ in.) [see p. 95]

For the 1992 "Documenta" exhibition in Kassel, Germany, Gerhard Richter filled a room with abstract paintings. In their midst, he placed a single Photo Painting, a still life of flowers. He repeated that strategy the next year in a show at the Marian Goodman Gallery, New York. There, in a space dominated by monumental abstractions, Richter hung this close-up view of cut yellow and white daisies and lilies seen against a two-toned gray and blue-gray ground.

The inclusion of a single Photo Painting among a group of abstract works highlighted the duality of Richter's practice. The fact that it is a floral still life underscored the oppositional nature of that duality. Abstractions and still life seemed to perform a mutual critique by calling into question the assumptions and desires underlying both modes. The generic prettiness of *Flowers* made the monumental abstractions appear grandiloquent, even strained, in their suggestion of meaning and emotion through sweeping gesture and intense coloration. By contrast *Flowers* offered an apparently simple statement of visual delight afforded by representation. The ambition of the abstractions, however, threw into relief the triviality of the floral still life. To find oneself captivated by this beautiful object seemed a guilty pleasure.

In 1970 and 1975, Richter made a number of photographs of flowers, which appear in his compendium of photographic images, *Atlas.*[1] These were taken outdoors and feature flowers growing in their natural environments. Richter did not use the motif in his paintings until almost twenty years later—the 1992 "Documenta" painting and the present work constitute the only instances of its appearance in the artist's painted oeuvre. In a 1993 interview with the curator Hans Ulrich Obrist, Richter suggested that the 1992 *Flowers* may have been inspired by a trip he made to Japan.[2] Asked if the flower pieces might become a cycle, Richter replied:

I have tried painting photographs of flowers since then, but there's nothing suitable. And when I tried to paint the flowers themselves, that didn't work either. Unfortunately, I should have remembered that it hardly ever works for me to take a photograph in order to use it for a painting. You take a photograph for its own sake, and then later, if you're lucky, you discover it as the source for a picture. It seems to be more a matter of chance, taking a shot with a specific quality that's worth painting.[3]

In the same interview, the two flower paintings occasioned a revealing exchange on the relationship of representation to nature:

Obrist: The flower pieces in particular raise the issue of the experiential reality of Nature, which is no longer a direct experience of Nature.
Richter: Because the flowers are cut and stuck into a vase—
Obrist: —or because it happens via the photograph.
Richter: I think that's less important, because directly painted flowers would be no less artificial. Everything is artificial. The bunch of flowers, the photograph—it's all artificial. There's nothing new about that. . . .

We make our own Nature, because we always see it in the way that suits us culturally. When we look on mountains as beautiful, although they're nothing but stupid and obstructive rock piles; or see that silly weed out there as a beautiful shrub, gently waving in the breeze: these are just our own projections, which go far beyond any practical, utilitarian values.[4]

With *Flowers* the limited, conventional nature of those projections is made powerfully, even painfully, evident. **J. S.**

Felix Gonzalez-Torres (CUBAN; 1957–1996)

Untitled (Last Light), 1993

Twenty-four light bulbs, plastic light sockets, extension cord, and dimmer switch; dimensions variable [see p. 90]

Felix Gonzalez-Torres used ordinary materials to extraordinary ends. From 1986 until his early death at the age of thirty-nine in 1996, he produced work of uncompromising beauty and simplicity, transforming everyday objects into profound meditations on love and loss. Perhaps nothing in the artist's oeuvre better exemplifies the quiet, elegiac nature of his project than a series of sculptural works made entirely of illuminated strings of light.

Untitled (Last Light) is a strand of twenty-four white light bulbs in brown plastic sockets placed at six-inch intervals on a twenty-four-foot, brown extension cord with a simple electrical wall plug.[1] Throughout his career, Gonzalez-Torres made more than twenty light-string works.[2] Apart from the number of bulbs in each piece and their vaguely referential parenthetical titles, the only variations from work to work result from installation, the specifics of which the artist insisted on leaving to the discretion of the respective owners. As a result, these pieces have been presented in a variety of configurations on gallery walls, floors, ceilings, as well as out of doors.

Gonzalez-Torres's conceptual program relies on a range of commonly held associations with strands of light. On one level, the lights have the potential to evoke the pleasures of a summer garden party, the joy of a holiday celebration, or the romance of a nightclub dance floor. The ephemeral nature of the materials, however, imbues the work with a certain melancholy. Light bulbs after all do not last forever. Over the course of any given installation, some of the bulbs are sure to burn out. Although the loss is both constant and inevitable, the extinguished lights are immediately replaced with new bulbs. The meaning of the piece depends on this invisible cycle and of course on the implicit metaphors for death and renewal.

It is no coincidence that *Untitled (Last Light)* contains an even number of bulbs, easily divided into twelve pairs and read as a reflection on couples. In many ways, all of Gonzalez-Torres's light works extend an examination of coupling and mortality that the artist began in 1987 with the first edition of *Untitled (Perfect Lovers)*. The "perfect lovers" are represented by a pair of identical, battery-operated wall clocks that are synchronized to keep the same time. (In both

series, there is no mistaking the nature of the couples: the clocks and the lights are identical to one another, and therefore refer to same-sex partners.) Inevitably, one of the batteries will begin to lose power before the other. Before long a subtle difference in the time becomes legible as one clock begins to slow. Eventually, one clock "dies" before the other. This piece, which Gonzalez-Torres made in response to the initial HIV-positive diagnosis of his lover, Ross Laycock, locates the "perfection" of the union in the ready potential for perpetual renewal: the batteries, like light bulbs, are easily replaced. The artist's first use of light bulbs can be traced to *Untitled (March 5th)* from 1991—the year Laycock died from AIDS-related illness. This first light sculpture, intended as a memorial of their relationship, consists simply of two bare bulbs suspended from entwined extension cords and titled in honor of Laycock's birthday. The poignant beauty of this fragile, artificial ecology extends throughout all of Gonzalez-Torres's mature work. **J. E. R.**

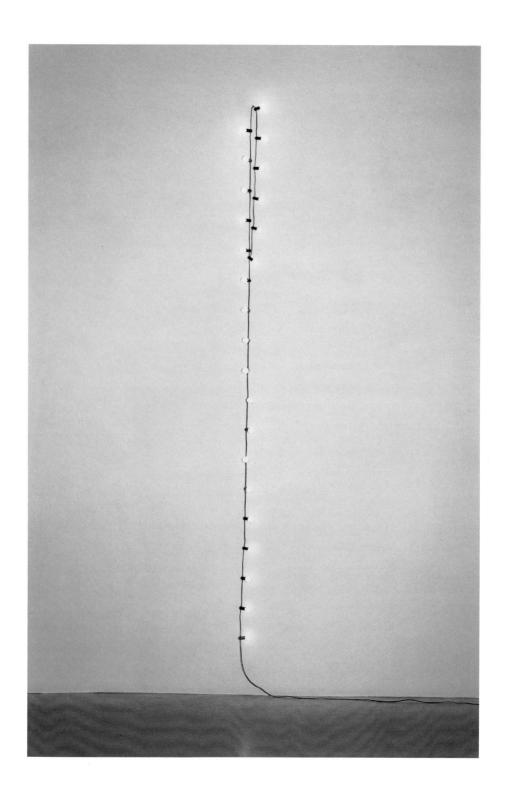

Checklist of the Lannan Collection STEPHANIE SKESTOS

The checklist includes all works accessioned as purchases and gifts of Lannan Foundation.
Dimensions are listed with height preceding width preceding depth, unless otherwise noted.

John Ahearn (AMERICAN; BORN 1951)

1 *Red Peanut,* 1980
Acrylic on cast plaster
38.4 x 44.1 x 10.8 cm
(15⅛ x 17⅜ x 4¼ in.)
Gift of Lannan Foundation, 1997.131
(pp. 52–53)

Carl Andre (AMERICAN; BORN 1935)

2 *Word Poem,* 1967
Ink and paper on painted cardboard tube
49.9 x 1.9 cm
(19⅛ x ¾ in.)
Gift of Lannan Foundation, 1997.132

Richard Artschwager (AMERICAN; BORN 1924)

3 *Table with Pink Tablecloth,* 1964
Formica on wood
64.8 x 111.8 x 111.8 cm
(25½ x 44 x 44 in.)
Gift of Lannan Foundation, 1997.133
(pp. 26–27)

Jonathan Borofsky (AMERICAN; BORN 1942)

4 *Hammering Man at 2,683,117,*
1977–80
Painted wood and metal with motor
and cables
348 x 144.8 x 33 cm
(137 x 57 x 13 in.)
Gift of Lannan Foundation, 1997.134

Scott Burton (AMERICAN; 1939–1989)

5 *Bronze Chair,* designed 1972,
cast 1975
Bronze
121.9 x 45.7 x 50.8 cm
(48 x 18 x 20 in.)
Gift of Lannan Foundation, 1997.136
(pp. 46–47)

6 *Aluminum Chair,* 1980–81
Aluminum and lacquer
76.2 x 59.7 x 177.8 cm
(30 x 23½ x 70 in.)
Gift of Lannan Foundation, 1997.135

7 *Low Piece (Bench),* 1985–86
Himalayan blue granite
43.2 x 121.9 x 45.7 cm
(17 x 48 x 18 in.)
Gift of Lannan Foundation, 1997.137

Vija Celmins (AMERICAN; BORN LATVIA, 1938)

8 *Explosion at Sea,* 1966
Oil on canvas
34.3 x 59.7 cm
(13½ x 23½ in.)
Gift of Lannan Foundation, 1997.138
(pp. 30–31)

9 *Untitled (Ocean),* 1968
Graphite on paper
32.4 x 44.5 cm
(12¾ x 17½ in.)
Gift of Lannan Foundation, 1997.106

Chuck Close (AMERICAN; BORN 1940)

  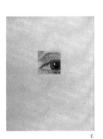

a   b   c

d   e

10 *Linda/Eye Series IV,* 1977
Series of five watercolors on paper
Each 76.2 x 57.2 cm
(30 x 22½ in.)
Gift of Lannan Foundation,
1997.107.1–5

a) *Linda/Eye Series I (Magenta),*
1977
Gift of Lannan Foundation, 1997.107.1
b) *Linda/Eye Series II (Cyan),* 1977
Gift of Lannan Foundation, 1997.107.2
c) *Linda/Eye Series III (Magenta and Cyan),* 1977
Gift of Lannan Foundation, 1997.107.3
d) *Linda/Eye Series IV (Yellow),* 1977
Gift of Lannan Foundation, 1997.107.4
e) *Linda/Eye Series V (Magenta, Cyan, and Yellow),* 1977
Gift of Lannan Foundation, 1997.107.5

Chuck Close (CONT.)

11 *Alex,* 1987
Internal dye-diffusion transfer print
(Polaroid) mounted on aluminum
78.7 x 55.9 cm
(31 x 22 in.)
William H. Bartels and Max V.
Kohnstamm prize funds; Katharine
Kuh and Marguerita S. Ritman
estates; gift of Lannan Foundation,
1997.226

12 *Maquette for "Alex,"* 1987
Internal dye-diffusion transfer print
(Polaroid) with tape and ink mounted
on foamcore
50.8 x 61 cm
(20 x 24 in.)
William H. Bartels and Max V.
Kohnstamm prize funds; Katharine
Kuh and Marguerita S. Ritman
estates; gift of Lannan Foundation,
1997.227

13 *Alex,* 1991
Oil on canvas
254 x 213.4 cm
(100 x 84 in.)
William H. Bartels and Max V.
Kohnstamm prize funds; Katharine
Kuh and Marguerita S. Ritman
estates; gift of Lannan Foundation,
1997.165
(pp. 74–75)

14 *Alex,* 1991
Color woodcut on paper
Block: 59.2 x 49.2 cm
(23¼ x 19⅜ in.);
sheet: 71.1 x 59.8 cm
(28 x 23⅕ in.)
William H. Bartels and Max V.
Kohnstamm prize funds; Katharine
Kuh and Marguerita S. Ritman estates;
gift of Lannan Foundation, 1997.316

state proofs

15 *Alex/Reduction Prints,* 1991–93
Fourteen screenprints from a
linoleum reduction block on paper
Each 182.9 x 147.3 cm
(79¾ x 69¼ in.)
William H. Bartels and Max V.
Kohnstamm prize funds; Katharine
Kuh and Marguerita S. Ritman
estates; gift of Lannan Foundation,
1997.317.1–14
(pp. 76–77)

progressive proofs

Chuck Close (CONT.)

16 *Alex*, 1992
Color woodcut on paper
Block: 59.7 x 49.6 cm
(23½ x 19½ in.);
sheet: 72.5 x 58.7 cm
(28 ½ x 23⅛ in.)
William H. Bartels and Max V.
Kohnstamm prize funds; Katharine
Kuh and Marguerita S. Ritman
estates; gift of Lannan Foundation,
1997.318

Jay DeFeo (AMERICAN; 1929–1989)

17 *The Annunciation*, 1957–59
Oil on canvas
306.7 x 189.2 cm
(120¾ x 74½ in.)
Gift of Lannan Foundation, 1997.139
(pp. 18–19)

Vernon Fisher (AMERICAN; BORN 1943)

18 *Interruption in a Field*, 1986
Acrylic and oil on canvas
207 x 276.9 cm
(81½ x 109 in.)
Gift of Lannan Foundation, 1997.140

Lucio Fontana (ITALIAN; BORN ARGENTINA, 1899–1968)

19 *Untitled*, c. 1964
Torn and scratched paper
50.2 x 59.1 cm
(19⅜ x 23¼ in.)
Gift of Lannan Foundation, 1997.108

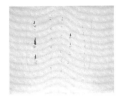

20 *Untitled*, c. 1964
Torn and scratched paper
50.2 x 59.1 cm
(19⅜ x 23¼ in.)
Gift of Lannan Foundation, 1997.109

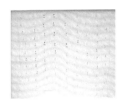

21 *Untitled*, c. 1964
Torn and scratched paper
50.2 x 59.1 cm
(19⅜ x 23¼ in.)
Gift of Lannan Foundation, 1997.110

Sam Francis (AMERICAN; 1923–1994)

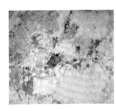

22 *In Lovely Blueness*, 1955–56
Oil on canvas
309.9 x 365.8 cm
(122 x 144 in.)
Mr. and Mrs. Frank G. Logan and
Flora Mayer Witkowsky prize
funds; through prior gifts of Wallace
DeWolf, A. A. Munger, and the
Charles H. and Mary F. S. Worcester
Collection; gift of Lannan Foundation,
1997.159
(pp. 16–17)

Tom Friedman (AMERICAN; BORN 1965)

23 *Untitled*, 1993
String
90.2 x 81.3 x 81.3 cm
(35½ x 32 x 32 in.)
Gift of Lannan Foundation, 1997.141
(pp. 80–81)

Felix Gonzalez-Torres (CUBAN; 1957–1996)

24 *Untitled (Last Light),* 1993
Twenty-four light bulbs, plastic
light sockets, extension cord, and
dimmer switch
Dimensions variable; cord: l. 731 cm
(288 in.)
Gift of Lannan Foundation, 1997.155
(pp. 84–85)

David Hammons (AMERICAN; BORN 1943)

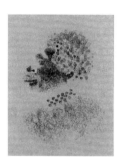

25 *American Costume,* 1970
Ink, powdered pigment, and fixative
on paper
62.2 x 49.2 cm
(24½ x 19⅜ in.)
Gift of Lannan Foundation, 1997.111
(pp. 42–43)

Keith Haring (AMERICAN; 1958–1990)

26 *Untitled,* 1981
Brush and black ink on two-ply board
46.4 x 61.3 cm
(18¼ x 24⅛ in.)
Gift of Lannan Foundation, 1997.112

27 *Untitled,* 1981
Fluorescent paint and sumi ink on
laminated canvas
174 x 243.2 cm
(68½ x 95¾ in.)
Gift of Lannan Foundation, 1997.142

Keith Haring (CONT.)

28 *Untitled (Vase),* 1981
Fiber-tipped pen on fiberglass
101 x 64.8 x 64.8 cm
(39¾ x 25½ x 25½ in.)
Gift of Lannan Foundation, 1997.368.1

29 *Untitled (Vase),* 1981
Fiber-tipped pen on fiberglass
101 x 64.8 x 64.8 cm
(39¾ x 25½ x 25½ in.)
Gift of Lannan Foundation, 1997.368.2

Eva Hesse (AMERICAN; BORN GERMANY, 1936–1970)

30 *Sequel,* 1967–68
Latex mixed with powdered
white pigment
Spheres: each diam. 6.7 cm
(2⅝ in.);
sheet: 76.2 x 81.3 cm
(30 x 32 in.)
Gift of Lannan Foundation, 1997.143

Gary Hill (AMERICAN; BORN 1951)

31 *Inasmuch As It Is Always Already
Taking Place,* 1990
Sixteen-channel video, sound installation with sixteen modified monitors
recessed in the wall
Niche: 40.6 x 137.2 x 167.6 cm
(16 x 54 x 66 in.)
Gift of Lannan Foundation, 1997.144
(pp. 72–73)

Alfredo Jaar (CHILEAN; BORN 1956)

32 *1 + 1 + 1*, 1987
Three sepia-toned transparencies in
light boxes, gilded frames, and mirror
127 x 487.7 x 182.9 cm
(50 x 192 x 72 in.)
Gift of Lannan Foundation, 1997.145
(pp. 58–59)

Alfred Jensen (AMERICAN; BORN GUATEMALA, 1903–1981)

33 *The Acroatic Rectangle, Per XIII,*
1967
Oil on canvas
182.9 x 149.9 cm
(72 x 59 in.)
Gift of Lannan Foundation, 1998.351
(pp. 32–33)

Bill Jensen (AMERICAN; BORN 1945)

34 *Drawing for Shamen*, 1975–76
Graphite and tempera on tracing paper
60.3 x 47.9 cm
(23¾ x 18⅞ in.)
Gift of Lannan Foundation, 1997.113

35 *Drawing for Magellan*, 1977
Graphite and oil, with smudging and
incising, on tracing paper
60.5 x 48.9 cm
(23¾ x 19¼ in.)
Gift of Lannan Foundation, 1997.114

Mike Kelley (AMERICAN; BORN 1954)

36 *Eviscerated Corpse*, 1989
Found stuffed animals, sewn together
Dimensions variable; approx.
177.8 x 254 x 421.6 cm
(70 x 100 x 166 in.)
Gift of Lannan Foundation, 1997.147
(pp. 66–67)

Sherrie Levine (AMERICAN; BORN 1947)

37 *Untitled (Check 2)*, 1985
Casein on mahogany panel
61 x 50.8 cm
(24 x 20 in.)
Gift of Lannan Foundation, 1997.148

Brice Marden (AMERICAN; BORN 1938)

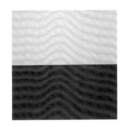

38 *Rodeo*, 1971
Oil and beeswax on two canvases
243.8 x 243.8 cm
(96 x 96 in.)
Ada S. Garrett Prize Fund; Katharine
Kuh Estate; through prior gift of
Mrs. Henry C. Woods; gift of Lannan
Foundation, 1997.160
(pp. 44–45)

39 *Ten Days*, 1971
Portfolio of eight etchings with other
media on paper
Gift of Lannan Foundation,
1997.115.1–8

a) Etching and aquatint in black ink
on paper
Plate: 39.6 x 52.5 cm
(15½ x 20⅝ in.);
sheet: 56 x 75.7 cm
(22⅛ x 29¾ in.)
Gift of Lannan Foundation, 1997.115.1

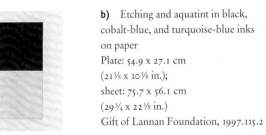

b) Etching and aquatint in black,
cobalt-blue, and turquoise-blue inks
on paper
Plate: 54.9 x 27.1 cm
(21⅝ x 10⅝ in.);
sheet: 75.7 x 56.1 cm
(29¾ x 22⅛ in.)
Gift of Lannan Foundation, 1997.115.2

c) Etching and aquatint in black
and silver inks on paper
Plate: 37.9 x 29.8 cm
(14⅞ x 11¾ in.);
sheet: 75.7 x 56.2 cm
(29¾ x 22⅛ in.)
Gift of Lannan Foundation, 1997.115.3

Brice Marden (CONT.)

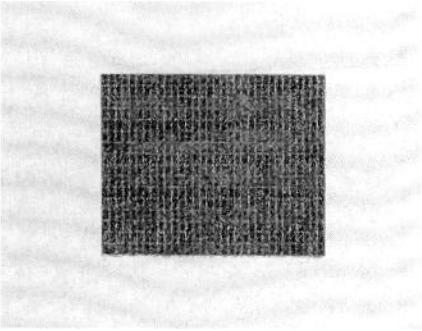

d) Etching in black ink on paper
Plate: 30.3 x 38 cm
(11 15/16 x 15 in.);
sheet: 56 x 75.4 cm
(22 1/8 x 29 5/8 in.)
Gift of Lannan Foundation, 1997.115.4

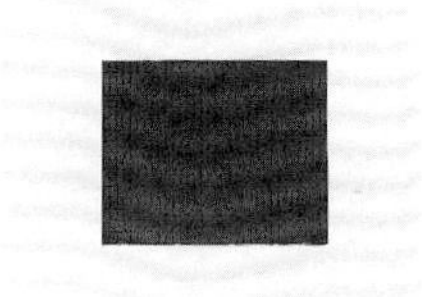

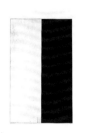

e) Etching and aquatint in black and silver-gray inks on paper
Plate: 30.3 x 38.3 cm
(11 15/16 x 15 in.);
sheet: 56.5 x 75.7 cm
(22 1/4 x 29 3/4 in.)
Gift of Lannan Foundation, 1997.115.5

f) Etching and aquatint in black ink on paper
Plate: 60 x 37 cm
(23 5/8 x 14 5/8 in.);
sheet: 75.7 x 56.2 cm
(21 7/8 x 22 1/8 in.)
Gift of Lannan Foundation, 1997.115.6

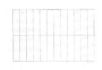

g) Etching and aquatint in black and burnt-umber inks on paper
Plate: 37 x 60 cm
(14 5/8 x 23 5/8 in.);
sheet: 56.2 x 75.7 cm
(22 1/8 x 29 3/4 in.)
Gift of Lannan Foundation, 1997.115.7

h) Etching in black and burnt-umber inks on paper
Plate: 37.3 x 60 cm
(14 5/8 x 23 5/8 in.);
sheet: 56.2 x 75.7 cm
(22 1/8 x 29 3/4 in.)
Gift of Lannan Foundation, 1997.115.8

Robert Morris (AMERICAN; BORN 1931)

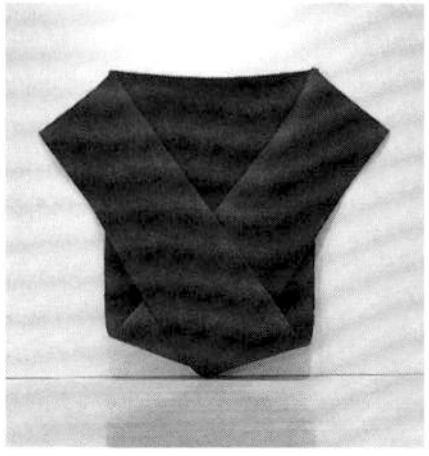

40 *Untitled,* 1976
Felt with metal grommets
261.6 x 294.6 x 58.4 cm
(103 x 116 x 23 in.)
Gift of Lannan Foundation, 1997.149

Robert Motherwell (AMERICAN; 1915–1991)

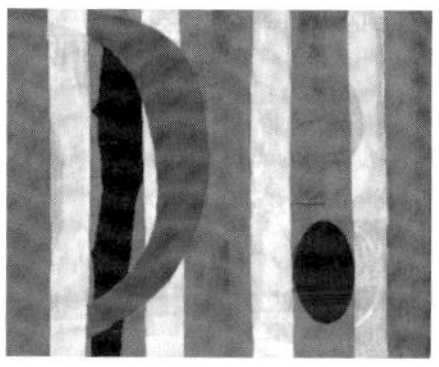

41 *Wall Painting with Stripes,* 1944
Oil on canvas
137.5 x 170.5 cm
(54 3/16 x 67 3/16 in.)
Gift of Muriel Kallis Steinberg Newman in honor of her grandchildren Ellen Steinberg and Peter Steinberg; gift of Lannan Foundation, 1997.161
(pp. 12–13)

Celia Alvarez Muñoz (AMERICAN; BORN 1937)

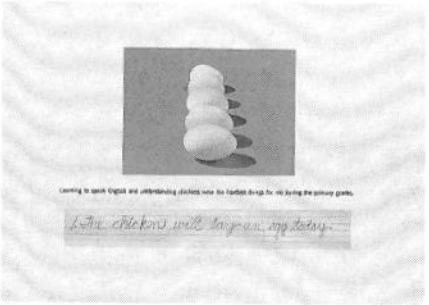

42 *Which Came First? (Enlightenment 4),* 1982
Embossed yellow box containing five rag-paper pages, including eight chromogenic color prints, ink, and graphite, with title page and colophon
Box: 34.3 x 50.8 x 3.2 cm (13 1/2 x 20 x 1 1/4 in.); pages: each 31.8 x 48.3 cm (12 1/2 x 19 in.); prints: each 12.7 x 17.8 cm (5 x 7 in.)
Gift of Lannan Foundation, 1997.267

Bruce Nauman (AMERICAN; BORN 1941)

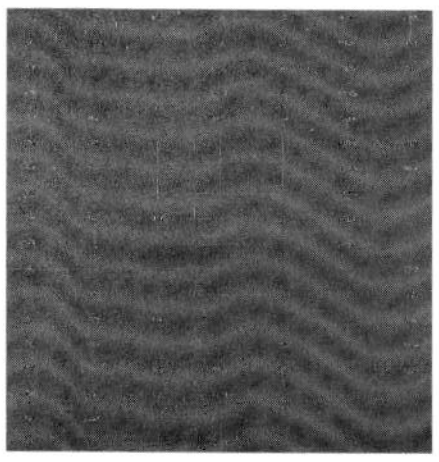

43 *Second Poem Piece,* 1969
Inscribed and stamped steel
152.3 x 152.4 x 1.3 cm
(60 x 60 x 1/2 in.)
Gift of Lannan Foundation, 1997.151
(pp. 38–39)

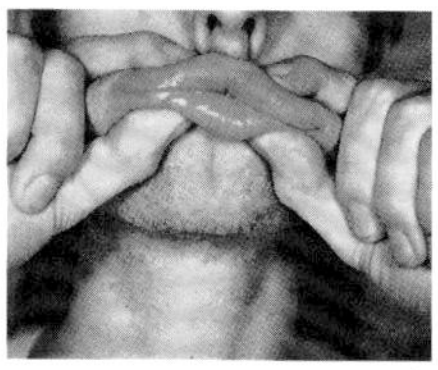
a

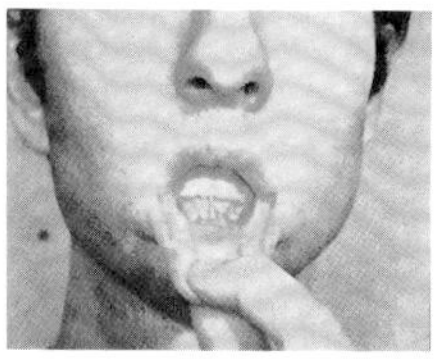
b

44 *Studies for Holograms,* 1970
Five screenprinted duotones on paper
Each 66 x 66 cm
(26 x 26 in.)
Gift of Lannan Foundation, 1997.116.1–5
(pp. 40–41)

a) *Pinched Lips,* 1970
Gift of Lannan Foundation, 1997.116.1

b) *Pulled Lower Lip,* 1970
Gift of Lannan Foundation, 1997.116.2

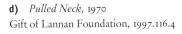

Bruce Nauman (CONT.)

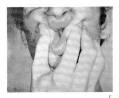

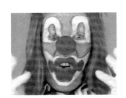

c) *Pinched Cheeks,* 1970
Gift of Lannan Foundation, 1997.116.3

d) *Pulled Neck,* 1970
Gift of Lannan Foundation, 1997.116.4

e) *Pulled Lips,* 1970
Gift of Lannan Foundation, 1997.116.5

45 *Good Boy Bad Boy,* 1985
Color video, sound
Dimensions variable
Gift of Lannan Foundation, 1997.162

46 *Clown Torture,* 1987
Color video, color-video projec-
tion, sound
Dimensions variable
Watson F. Blair Prize Fund; W. L.
Mead Endowment; Twentieth-Century
Purchase Fund; through prior gift of
Joseph Winterbotham; gift of Lannan
Foundation, 1997.162
(pp. 62–63)

Isamu Noguchi (AMERICAN; 1904–1988)

47 *Figure,* 1946
Georgia marble
168.3 x 49.5 x 38.1 cm
(66 ¼ x 19 ½ x 15 in.)
Alonzo C. Mather and Laura Slobe
Memorial prize funds; Marguerita S.
Ritman Estate; through prior gifts
of Helmuth Bartsch, Mr. and Mrs.
Martin A. Ryerson, and Solomon B.
Smith; gift of Lannan Foundation,
1997.166
(pp. 14–15)

Sigmar Polke (GERMAN; BORN 1941)

48 *Uri Geller Welcomes Unknown
Beings from the Realm of Fables
(Uri Geller empfängt fremde Wesen
aus der Fabel),* 1976
Three-part collage with mixed media
Prints: each 29.2 x 41.9 cm
(11 ½ x 16 ½ in.); primary mounts:
each 30.5 x 43.2 cm (12 x 17 in.)
Gift of Lannan Foundation,
1997.117.1–3
(pp. 50–51)

a) Gelatin silver print with newsprint collage
Gift of Lannan Foundation, 1997.117.2

b) Gelatin silver print with applied
color (ball-point and fiber-tipped pen)
and paper collage
Gift of Lannan Foundation, 1997.117.1

c) Gelatin silver print with
applied color (fiber-tipped pen) and
newsprint collage
Gift of Lannan Foundation, 1997.117.3

Ad Reinhardt (AMERICAN; 1913–1967)

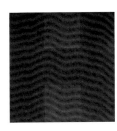

49 *Abstract Painting 1960–1965,*
1960–65
Oil on canvas
152.4 x 152.4 cm
(60 x 60 in.)
Emilie L. Wild Prize Fund; Marguerita
S. Ritman Estate; through prior acquisitions of Friends of American Art and
Mr. and Mrs. Carter H. Harrison; gift
of Lannan Foundation, 1997.163
(pp. 22–23)

Gerhard Richter (GERMAN; BORN 1932)

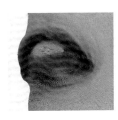

50 *Mouth (Mund),* 1963
Oil on canvas
67.3 x 74.3 cm
(26 ½ x 29 ¼ in.)
Through prior gift of Mrs. Henry C.
Woods; gift of Lannan Foundation,
1997.173
(pp. 24–25)

51 *Woman Descending the Staircase
(Frau die Treppe herabgehend)*, 1965
Oil on canvas
200.7 x 129.5 cm
(79 x 51 in.)
Roy J. and Frances R. Friedman
Endowment; gift of Lannan
Foundation, 1997.176
(pp. 28–29)

52 *Mrs. Wolleh with Children
(Frau Wolleh mit Kindern)*, 1968
Oil on canvas
200 x 160 cm
(78¾ x 63 in.)
Through prior gift of Mr. and
Mrs. Lewis Larned Coburn; gift
of Lannan Foundation, 1997.175
(pp. 34–35)

53 *9 Objects (9 Objekte)*, 1968
Nine photo-offset lithographs
on paper
Each 44.8 x 44.8 cm
(17⅛ x 17⅛ in.)
Through prior gift of Joseph
Winterbotham; gift of Lannan
Foundation, 1997.315.1–9
(pp. 36–37)

54 *Little Landscape by the Sea
(Kleine Landschaft am Meer)*, 1969
Oil on canvas
72.5 x 105.1 cm
(28½ x 41⅜ in.)
Through prior gift of Mr. and
Mrs. Lewis Larned Coburn; gift
of Lannan Foundation, 1997.171

55 *Candle (Kerze)*, 1982
Oil on canvas
69.9 x 54.6 cm
(27½ x 21½ in.)
Through prior gift of Mr. and
Mrs. Lewis Larned Coburn; gift
of Lannan Foundation, 1997.172

a

56 *Ice 1–4 (Eis 1–4)*, 1989
Four oil paintings on canvas
Each 203.2 x 162.6 cm
(80 x 64 in.)
Through prior gift of Joseph
Winterbotham; gift of Lannan
Foundation, 1997.167–70
(pp. 68–71)

b

a) *Ice 1 (Eis 1)*, 1989
Through prior gift of Joseph
Winterbotham; gift of Lannan
Foundation, 1997.167

b) *Ice 2 (Eis 2)*, 1989
Through prior gift of Joseph
Winterbotham; gift of Lannan
Foundation, 1997.168

c

c) *Ice 3 (Eis 3)*, 1989
Through prior gift of Joseph
Winterbotham; gift of Lannan
Foundation, 1997.169

d

d) *Ice 4 (Eis 4)*, 1989
Through prior gift of Joseph
Winterbotham; gift of Lannan
Foundation, 1997.170

Gerhard Richter (CONT.)

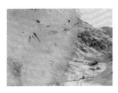

57 *17.3.92*, 1992
Acrylic on chromogenic color print
12.7 x 17.5 cm
(5 x 6 ⅞ in.)
Through prior gift of Joseph
Winterbotham; gift of Lannan
Foundation, 1997.312

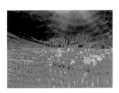

58 *19.3.92*, 1992
Acrylic on chromogenic color print
12.7 x 17.5 cm
(5 x 6 ⅞ in.)
Through prior gift of Joseph
Winterbotham; gift of Lannan
Foundation, 1997.313

59 *20.3.92*, 1992
Acrylic on chromogenic color print
12.7 x 17.5 cm
(5 x 6 ⅞ in.)
Through prior gift of Joseph
Winterbotham; gift of Lannan
Foundation, 1997.314

60 *Flowers (Blumen)*, 1993
Oil on canvas
72.5 x 102.2 cm
(28 ½ x 40 ¼ in.)
Through prior gift of Mrs. Henry C.
Woods; gift of Lannan Foundation,
1997.174
(pp. 82–83)

Thomas Ruff (GERMAN; BORN 1958)

61 *Untitled (Ralph Müller)*, 1986
Chromogenic color print in
artist's frame
205.1 x 163.2 cm
(80 ¾ x 63 ¼ in.)
Gift of Lannan Foundation, 1997.125
(p. 55)

62 *Untitled*, 1988
Chromogenic color print in
artist's frame
210.8 x 165.1 cm
(83 x 65 in.)
Gift of Lannan Foundation, 1997.126
(p. 56)

63 *Untitled*, 1988
Chromogenic color print in
artist's frame
210.2 x 165.4 cm
(82 ¾ x 65 ⅛ in.)
Gift of Lannan Foundation, 1997.127
(p. 57)

Allen Ruppersberg (AMERICAN; BORN 1944)

64 *Remainders: Novel, Sculpture,
Film*, 1991
One hundred twenty-eight hardcover
books with jackets on a wooden
table, five cardboard packing cartons,
and one signed paper bookmark
114.3 x 121.9 x 76.2 cm
(45 x 48 x 30 in.)
Gift of Lannan Foundation, 1997.152
(pp. 78–79)

Edward Ruscha (AMERICAN; BORN 1937)

65 *Smaller Dish,* 1985
Dry pigment on paper
101.6 x 152.4 cm
(40 x 60 in.)
Gift of Lannan Foundation, 1997.118

66 *F House,* 1987
Acrylic on canvas
116.8 x 203.2 cm
(46 x 80 in.)
Gift of Lannan Foundation, 1997.153
(pp. 60–61)

Lucas Samaras (AMERICAN; BORN GREECE, 1936)

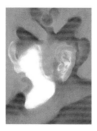

67 *Untitled—February 16, 1961,* 1961
Pastel on paper
30.7 x 22.8 cm
(12 1/16 x 8 15/16 in.)
Gift of Lannan Foundation, 1997.331
(fig. 1, p. 48)

68 *Untitled—Early November 1961,* 1961
Pastel on paper
30.7 x 22.8 cm
(12 1/16 x 8 15/16 in.)
Gift of Lannan Foundation, 1997.119

Lucas Samaras (CONT.)

69 *Phototransformation (10/25/73),* 1973
Internal dye-diffusion transfer print
(Polaroid)
7.6 x 7.6 cm
(3 x 3 in.)
Gift of Lannan Foundation, 1997.130
(p. 49)

70 *Phototransformation (4/4/76),* 1976
Internal dye-diffusion transfer print
(Polaroid)
7.6 x 7.6 cm
(3 x 3 in.)
Gift of Lannan Foundation, 1997.128
(p. 49)

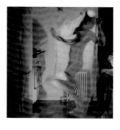

71 *Phototransformation (7/31/76),* 1976
Internal dye-diffusion transfer print
(Polaroid)
7.6 x 7.6 cm
(3 x 3 in.)
Gift of Lannan Foundation, 1997.129
(p. 49)

Joel Shapiro (AMERICAN; BORN 1941)

72 *34 Blows,* 1971
Copper
15.2 x 285.8 x 3.2 cm
(6 x 112 1/2 x 1 1/4 in.)
Gift of Lannan Foundation, 1997.154

Lorna Simpson (AMERICAN; BORN 1960)

73 *Untitled,* 1995
Color waterless lithograph on felt
39.5 x 38 cm
(12 x 15 in.)
Gift of Lannan Foundation, 1997.120

Kiki Smith (AMERICAN; BORN GERMANY, 1954)

74 *Untitled*, 1988
Ink on gampi paper
121.9 x 96.5 x 17.8 cm
(48 x 38 x 7 in.)
Gift of Lannan Foundation, 1997.121
(pp. 64–65)

Robert Smithson (AMERICAN; 1938–1973)

75 *Study for Earthwork Proposal*,
1969
Graphite, fiber-tipped pen, and colored
crayons on paper
45.1 x 61 cm
(17¾ x 24 in.)
Gift of Lannan Foundation, 1997.122

Clyfford Still (AMERICAN; 1904–1980)

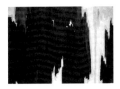

76 *Untitled*, 1958
Oil on canvas
292.2 x 406.4 cm
(114¼ x 160 in.)
Mr. and Mrs. Frank G. Logan Prize
Fund; Roy J. and Frances R. Friedman
Endowment; through prior gift of
Mrs. Henry C. Woods; gift of Lannan
Foundation, 1997.164
(pp. 20–21)

John Storrs (AMERICAN; 1885–1956)

77 *Female Icarus*, 1917
Etching on paper
11.3 x 8.6 cm
(4⁷⁄₁₆ x 3⅜ in.)
Gift of Lannan Foundation, 1997.123

Lenore Tawney (AMERICAN; BORN 1907)

78 *Untitled #32*, 1976
Wooden box covered with manuscript
pages, perforated and strung with linen
threads and nutshells
18 x 21.5 x 12.6 cm
(7⅛ x 8½ x 5 in.)
Gift of Lannan Foundation, 1997.358

79 *Untitled #34*, 1976
Wooden box covered with manuscript
pages and feathers
13.8 x 24.8 x 10.7 cm
(5½ x 9¾ x 4¼ in.)
Gift of Lannan Foundation, 1997.359

Robert Thompson (AMERICAN; 1937–1966)

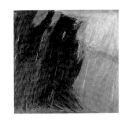

80 *Beach of Silenus*, 1964
Acrylic on paper with commercially
printed text
26.1 x 27.6 cm
(10¼ x 10⅞ in.)
Gift of Lannan Foundation, 1997.124

Jack Tworkov (AMERICAN; BORN POLAND, 1900–1982)

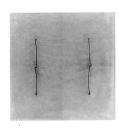

81 *Height*, 1958–59
Oil on canvas
194.3 x 183.5 cm
(76½ x 72¼ in.)
Gift of Lannan Foundation, 1997.156

Chris Wilmarth (AMERICAN; 1943–1987)

82 *Twice*, 1970
Acidized glass and steel wire
43.2 x 43.2 x 2.5 cm
(17 x 17 x 1 in.)
Gift of Lannan Foundation, 1997.157

Selected References and Notes

References are keyed to artists' names, in alphabetical order. Following the references, also under artists' names, notes to the entries appear below titles of works. In cases of multiple works by individual artists, titles are listed in chronological order.

AHEARN, JOHN

Houston, Contemporary Arts Museum. *South Bronx Hall of Fame: Sculpture by John Ahearn and Rigoberto Torres*. Exh. cat. by Richard Goldstein, Michael Ventura, and Marilyn A. Zeitlin. 1991.
Kramer, Janet. *Whose Art Is It?* Durham, N.C./London, 1994.
Portland, Ore., Reed College, Douglas F. Cooley Memorial Art Gallery. *Sculpture by John Ahearn and Rigoberto Torres: The South Bronx Hall of Fame and Other Realities*. Exh. brochure by Susan Fillin-Yeh. 1993.
Schwartzman, Allan. *Street Art*. Garden City, N.Y., 1985. Pp. 78–97.

Red Peanut, 1980, pp. 52–53

1. Stephan Eins established Fashion Moda in 1978 in a storefront space in the South Bronx. He intended the gallery to be:

> a place for art, science, invention, technology and fantasy. The philosophy of Fashion Moda is based on the premise that art/creativity can happen anywhere. It can be made and appreciated by people who are known and unknown, trained and untrained, middle class and poor. Fashion Moda has created a situation where local artists and residents can interrelate with downtown, national and international art community to exchange ideas and share energies (Schwartzman, p. 78).

2. Notes from Ahearn's visit to the Lannan Foundation, Los Angeles, Nov. 15, 1989.

ARTSCHWAGER, RICHARD

Buffalo, Albright-Knox Art Gallery, et al. *Richard Artschwager's Theme(s)*. Exh. cat. 1979.
Celant, Germano. "Richard Artschwager's Concrete Mirages." In Madison, Wis., University of Wisconsin, Elvehjem Museum of Art. *Richard Artschwager, public (public)*. Exh. cat. by Russell Panczenko et al. 1991. Pp. 9–15.
McDevitt, Jan. "The Object: Still Life." *Craft Horizons* 25 (Sept.–Oct. 1965), pp. 28–30, 54.
Madoff, Steven Henry. "Richard Artschwager's Sleight of Mind." *ARTnews* 87 (Jan. 1988), pp. 114–21.
New York, Whitney Museum of American Art. *Richard Artschwager*. Exh. cat. by Richard Armstrong. 1988.

Table with Pink Tablecloth, 1964, pp. 26–27

1. Artschwager, quoted in McDevitt, p. 30.

2. Madoff, p. 116.

BURTON, SCOTT

Baltimore, The Baltimore Museum of Art. *Scott Burton*. Exh. cat. by Brenda Richardson. 1986.
Düsseldorf, Kunstverein für die Rheinlande und Westfalen. *Scott Burton: Skulpturen 1980–89*. Exh. cat. by Jiri Svestka. 1989.
London, Tate Gallery. *Scott Burton*. Exh. cat. by Richard Francis. 1985.

Bronze Chair, designed 1972, cast 1975, pp. 46–47

1. Burton, quoted in Baltimore, p. 19. Queen Anne Revival style was popular from the 1860s through the early twentieth century in England and the United States. Developed in reaction to the Gothic Revival, Queen Anne Revival drew from Dutch-influenced design in England during the late seventeenth and eighteenth centuries.

2. The noted art patron Marion Stroud Swingle, who briefly owned the piece before returning it to the artist, paid the $5,000 cost of fabrication. In 1979 Burton made a pastiche cast of the *Bronze Chair* called *Bronze Chair (Replica)*, now in the Allen Memorial Art Museum, Oberlin College, Oberlin, Ohio.

3. *Bronze Chair* can be read for example in light of a later, unrealized proposal for a public park in Smithtown, New York. In 1976 Burton designed an outdoor environment based upon the popular vernacular of a middle-class American living room. The artist envisioned the standard wall-to-wall carpet as a manicured lawn, on which he would place common versions of Victorian and Chippendale reproduction-furniture cast in bronze.

4. In 1991 the Estate of Scott Burton, following the stipulations of the artist's will, offered The Art Institute of Chicago the opportunity to purchase *Bronze Chair* at roughly half its current market value, after The Museum of Modern Art, New York (cobeneficiary of the estate), declined to acquire the piece. Charles F. Stuckey, then Curator of Twentieth-Century Painting and Sculpture at the Art Institute and a longtime supporter of Burton, embarked on a spirited, grassroots campaign to raise money for the acquisition. A wide range of Burton's friends, supporters, and admirers made contributions in large and small amounts. Ultimately, Lannan Foundation agreed to acquire the piece, promising that it would enter the museum's collection no later than January 1, 2000. The thousands of dollars raised were returned to the individual donors, and *Bronze Chair* came to the Art Institute in 1997 as part of the foundation's larger gift of objects.

CELMINS, VIJA

Los Angeles, Newport Harbor Art Museum. *Vija Celmins: A Survey Exhibition*. Exh. cat. by Betty Turnbull. 1979.
Philadelphia, Institute of Contemporary Art. *Vija Celmins*. Exh. cat. by Judith Tannenbaum. 1992.
Princethal, Nancy. "Vija Celmins: Material Fictions." *Parkett* 44 (1995), pp. 25–28.
Relyea, Lane. "Earth to Vija Celmins." *Artforum* 32 (Oct. 1993), pp. 55–59, 115.

Explosion at Sea, 1966, pp. 30–31

1. Philadelphia, p. 15.

2. According to David McKee (McKee to Lisa Lyons of Lannan Foundation, Los Angeles, 1992), *Explosion at Sea* is based on a photograph of an unsuccessful Kamikaze pilot attack on a United States aircraft carrier, the *Suwannee*, which took place in October 1944 in the Pacific theater of World War II.

3. On the relationship of the series to Celmins's childhood, see Los Angeles; and Los Angeles, Museum of Contemporary Art, *Vija Celmins*, exh. brochure (1993).

4. Celmins, quoted in Philadelphia, p. 15.

CLOSE, CHUCK

Close, Chuck. *The Portraits Speak: Chuck Close in Conversation with 27 of His Subjects.* New York, 1997.
Guare, John. *Chuck Close: Life and Work, 1988–1995.* New York, 1995.
Lyons, Lisa, and Robert Storr. *Chuck Close.* New York, 1987.
Minneapolis, Walker Art Center. *Close Portraits.* Exh. cat. by Lisa Lyons and Martin Friedman. 1980.
New York, The Museum of Modern Art, et al. *Chuck Close.* Exh. cat. by Robert Storr et al. 1998.

Alex, 1991, pp. 74–75

1. The Lannan Collection contains several objects related to the 1991 *Alex* painting, including a Polaroid of Alex Katz (Checklist no. 11) and a Polaroid used as a maquette (Checklist no. 12).

2. Close, pp. 316–17.

3. Both paintings actually contain a range of blues and browns despite their grisaille effect.

4. Close, p. 319.

5. Ibid.

Alex/Reduction Prints, 1991–93, pp. 76–77

1. Linoleum was originally composed of linseed oil, cork, and binding agents. It is much easier to cut into than modern synthetic linoleums, which are all plastic-based. Battleship linoleum, which dates back to the turn of the twentieth century, came in huge sheets used for the decks of ships. Linoleum manufactured with the original formula is hard to find nowadays, but especially so in battleship-sized sheets.

2. Deborah Wye, "Changing Expressions: Printmaking," in New York, p. 80.

DEFEO, JAY

Berkeley, University of California, University Art Museum. *Jay DeFeo: Works on Paper.* Exh. cat. by Sidra Stich. 1989.
New York, Whitney Museum of American Art. *Beat Culture and the New America: 1950–1965.* Exh. cat. 1995.
Philadelphia, Moore College of Art and Design, Goldie Paley Gallery. *Jay DeFeo: Selected Works 1952–1989.* Exh. cat. 1996.

San Francisco, Museo ItaloAmericano. *Jay DeFeo: The Florence View and Related Works 1950–1954.* Exh. cat. with essays by Klaus Kertess, Constance Lewallen, and Robert A. Whyte. 1997.
San Francisco, San Francisco Art Institute. *Jay DeFeo: Selected Works, Past and Present.* Exh. cat. by Thomas Albright and David S. Rubin. 1984.

The Annunciation, 1957–59, pp. 18–19

1. Philadelphia, p. 11.

2. DeFeo to J. Patrick Lannan, Sr., 1959; published in ibid., pp. 12–13.

FRANCIS, SAM

Paris, Galerie nationale du Jeu de Paume. *Sam Francis, les années parisiennes, 1950–1961.* Exh. cat. 1995.
Selz, Peter. *Sam Francis.* Rev. ed. New York, 1982.

In Lovely Blueness, 1955–56, pp. 16–17

1. Francis, quoted in Selz, p. 20.

2. Friedrich Hölderlin, *Hymns and Fragments*, trans. by Richard Sieburth (Princeton, N.J., 1984), p. 249.

FRIEDMAN, TOM

Chicago, The Art Institute of Chicago. *Affinities: Chuck Close and Tom Friedman.* Exh. brochure by Madeleine Grynsztejn. 1996.
New York, The Museum of Modern Art. *Projects 50: Tom Friedman.* Exh. cat. and interview by Robert Storr. 1995.
St. Louis, The Saint Louis Art Museum. *Currents 70: Tom Friedman.* Exh. cat. by Rochelle Steiner. 1997.

Untitled, 1993, pp. 80–81

1. Friedman started with a small, glue-infused core of stiffened string, so that the work would withstand the rigors of being moved.

2. According to Friedman, the connection to "Cousin It" pleases him not only for the linguistic suggestion of vagueness carried by the name and subject, but also for the somewhat corny humor and pop familiarity of the television show. Friedman, conversation with author, Mar. 8, 1999.

3. Ibid.

GONZALEZ-TORRES, FELIX

Gonzalez-Torres, Felix. *Felix Gonzalez-Torres.* Interview by Tim Rollins; essay by Susan Cahan; short story by Jan Avgikos. New York, 1993.
Graz, Switzerland, Neue Galerie Graz. *Felix Gonzalez-Torres, Rudolf Stingel.* Exh. cat. by Jan Avgikos. 1994.
Hannover, Sprengel Museum, et al. *Felix Gonzalez-Torres.* 2 vols. Exh. cat. and cat. rais. by Dietmar Elger. Ostfildern-Ruit/New York, 1997.
Los Angeles, Museum of Contemporary Art. *Felix Gonzalez-Torres.* Exh. cat. 1994.
Munich, Sammlung Goetz. *Felix Gonzalez-Torres, Roni Horn.* Exh. cat. 1995.
New York, Solomon R. Guggenheim Museum. *Felix Gonzalez-Torres.* Exh. cat. by Nancy Spector. 1995.

Untitled (Last Light), 1993, pp. 84–85

1. The original specifications for the bulbs are as follows: ABCO, ten watt, candelabra base, satin white, globe size G9, model #03864. The certificate for the piece reads: "If these exact bulbs are not available, a similar bulb of the same wattage may be used." Gonzalez-Torres allowed the addition of approximately twelve and one-half extra feet of cord at the end closest to the plug for installation purposes. He also stated that the light strands may be exhibited with all the bulbs turned off.

2. The majority of Gonzalez-Torres's light strings contain forty-two bulbs. There are exceptions: *Untitled (North)* of 1993 consists of twelve light strings with twenty-two bulbs each and *Untitled (Arena)* of 1993 has sixty bulbs. *Untitled* and *Untitled (Silver)*, both of 1992, and *Untitled (Last Light)* are the only pieces with a total of twenty-four bulbs each.

HAMMONS, DAVID

Blazwick, Iwona, and Emma Dexter. "Rich in Ruins." *Parkett* 31 (1992), pp. 26–33.

Jones, Kellie. "The Structure of Myth and the Potency of Magic." In *David Hammons: Rousing the Rubble*. New York, 1991. Pp. 14–37.

Papastergiadis, Nikos. "David Hammons." In Cambridge, Eng., Kettle's Yard. *Re-writing History*. Exh. cat. ed. by Anna Harding. 1990. Pp. 21–22.

American Costume, 1970, pp. 42–43

1. Other examples of Hammons's body prints include *3 Spades* (1971; private collection), which depicts a black man in profile holding a large spade under his arm and a smaller one in his left hand; and the powerful *Injustice Case* (1973; Los Angeles County Museum of Art), in which an American flag serves as the background for an image of a black man in profile, seated in a chair, and tied up. The latter work was inspired by the 1969 Chicago Eight trial, at which the defendant Bobby Seale was bound and gagged.

2. The Works Progress Administration facilitated the implementation of a nationwide, public arts program by employing American artists during the Great Depression.

3. The term "Other" has been employed in the post-modern era as a reference for entities outside of the "Self." It has been commonly used as a label for distinguishing what is alien from what is familiar; for example from a Eurocentric point of view, it might set apart the non-Western from the Western, the non-white from the white, the foreign from the local, etc.

4. Hammons's use of found objects connects his work to twentieth-century artistic movements such as Dada, Arte Povera, and Outsider Art.

HILL, GARY

Liverpool, Tate Gallery, et al. *Gary Hill: In Light of the Other*. Exh. cat. 1993.

Seattle, University of Washington, Henry Art Gallery. *Gary Hill*. Exh. cat. 1994.

Valencia, IVAM Centre del carme. *Gary Hill*. Exh. cat. 1993.

Inasmuch As It Is Always Already Taking Place, 1990, pp. 72–73

1. Gary Hill, "Inasmuch As It Is Always Already Taking Place," in Copenhagen, Ny Carlsberg Glyptotek, *Other Words and Images: Video af Gary Hill*, exh. cat. (1990), p. 27.

JAAR, ALFREDO

Barcelona, Centre d'Art Santa Mònica, et al. *Let There be Light. The Rwanda Project, 1994–1998*. 2 vols. Exh. cat. by Alfredo Jaar et al. 1998.

Jaar, Alfredo. *It is Difficult. Ten Years.* Essay by Rick Pirro. Barcelona, 1998.

La Jolla, Calif., La Jolla Museum of Contemporary Art. *Alfredo Jaar*. Exh. cat. by Madeleine Grynsztejn. 1990.

Richmond, Va., Virginia Commonwealth University, Anderson Gallery, et al. *Alfredo Jaar: Geography = War*. Exh. cat. with essays by W. Avon Drake, Steven S. High, H. Ashley Kistler, and Adriana Valdés. 1991.

JENSEN, ALFRED

Basel, Kunsthalle Basel. *Alfred Jensen*. Exh. cat. by Arnold Rudlinger. 1964.

Bern, Kunsthalle Bern. *Alfred Jensen*. Exh. cat. by Wieland Schmied. 1973.

Buffalo, Albright-Knox Art Gallery. *Alfred Jensen: Paintings and Diagrams from the Years 1957–1977*. Exh. cat. with essays by Linda L. Cathcart and Marcia Tucker. 1978.

New York, Pace Gallery. *Alfred Jensen: The Late Works*. Exh. cat. 1983.

New York, Solomon R. Guggenheim Museum. *Alfred Jensen: Paintings and Works on Paper*. Exh. cat. 1985.

The Acroatic Rectangle, Per XIII, 1967, pp. 32–33

1. Jensen had had his first solo exhibition in New York in 1952, at the John Heller Gallery.

2. Buffalo, p. 91.

3. Most of the other paintings from the series are in private collections, although examples are held by the Whitney Museum of American Art, New York, and the Albright-Knox Art Gallery, Buffalo.

4. Regina Bogat Jensen, the artist's wife, fax to author, June 9, 1998.

KELLEY, MIKE

Barcelona, Museu d'Art Contemporani de Barcelona, et al. *Mike Kelley: 1985–1996*. Exh. cat. ed. by M. Angeles Lopez and Elisenda Prat; trans. by Gloria Bohigas. 1997.

Bartman, William S., and Miyoshi Barosh, eds. *Mike Kelley*. Interview by John Miller. New York, 1992.

Basel, Kunsthalle Basel, et al. *Mike Kelley*. Exh. cat. by Thomas Kellein et al. 1992.

Chicago, University of Chicago, Renaissance Society. *Mike Kelley: Three Projects: Half a Man, From My Institution to Yours, Pay For Your Pleasure*. Exh. cat. 1988.

New York, Whitney Museum of American Art, et al. *Mike Kelley, Catholic Tastes*. Exh. cat. by Elisabeth Sussman, with contributions by Richard Armstrong et al. 1993.

Eviscerated Corpse, 1989, pp. 66–67

1. Kelley, quoted in Ralph Rugoff, "Dirty Toys: Mike Kelley Interviewed," in Basel, p. 86.

2. Howard Fox, "Artist in Exile," in New York, p. 191.

3. Kelley, quoted in Washington, D.C., Hirshhorn Museum and Sculpture Garden, *Directions/Mike Kelley: Half a Man*, exh. brochure by Amanda Cruz (1991), n. p.

MARDEN, BRICE

Houston, Rice University, Institute for the Arts. *Marden, Novros, Rothko: Painting in the Age of Actuality.* Exh. cat. by Sheldon Nodelman. 1978.

Kertess, Klaus. *Brice Marden: Paintings and Drawings.* New York, 1992.

London, Tate Gallery. *Brice Marden: Prints, 1961–1991: A Catalogue Raisonné.* Exh. cat. and cat. rais. by Jeremy Lewison. 1992.

New York, Dia Center for the Arts. *Brice Marden—Cold Mountain.* Exh. cat. by Brenda Richardson. 1992.

MOTHERWELL, ROBERT

Arnason, H. Harvard, et al. *Motherwell.* 2d ed. New York, 1982.

Buffalo, Albright-Knox Art Gallery, et al. *Robert Motherwell.* Exh. cat. by Dore Ashton and Jack D. Flam; intro. by Robert T. Buck. 1983.

Mattison, Robert Saltonstall. *Robert Motherwell: The Formative Years.* Ann Arbor, 1987.

Motherwell, Robert. *The Collected Writings of Robert Motherwell.* Ed. by Stephanie Terenzio. New York/Oxford, 1992.

New York, The Museum of Modern Art, et al. *Robert Motherwell.* Exh. cat. by Frank O'Hara. 1965.

Wall Painting with Stripes, 1944, p. 12–13

1. A photograph by Peter A. Juley and Sons shows Motherwell at work in his New York studio; an unfinished *Wall Painting with Stripes* stands on an easel next to the artist. The photograph has been dated in various publications from 1943 to 1945. *Wall Painting with Stripes* seems to have been shown publicly for the first time at a one-person exhibition at the Arts Club of Chicago in 1946.

2. "Fat" paint is loaded with oil and dries very slowly; "thin" paint is cut with turpentine and dries more quickly.

NAUMAN, BRUCE

Bruggen, Coosje van. *Bruce Nauman.* New York, 1988.

Cordes, Christopher, ed. *Bruce Nauman, Prints 1970–89.* Cat. rais. New York/Chicago, 1989.

London, Hayward Gallery. *Bruce Nauman.* Exh. cat. with essays by François Albera, Christine van Assche, Vincent Labaume, Jean Charles Masséra, and Gijs van Tuyl. 1998.

London, Whitechapel Art Gallery. *Bruce Nauman.* Exh. cat. with essays by Jean Christophe Ammann, Nicholas Serota, and Joan Simon. 1986.

Los Angeles, Los Angeles County Museum of Art, et al. *Bruce Nauman: Work from 1965 to 1972.* Exh. cat. by Jane Livingston and Marcia Tucker. 1972.

Minneapolis, Walker Art Center, et al. *Bruce Nauman.* Exh. cat. and cat. rais. with essays by Neal Benezra, Kathy Halbreich, Paul Schimmel, Joan Simon, and Robert Storr. 1994.

Second Poem Piece, 1969, pp. 38–39

1. Neal Benezra, "Surveying Nauman," in Minneapolis, p. 29.

2. Nauman, quoted in Los Angeles, p. 44.

Studies for Holograms, 1970, pp. 40–41

1. Among these 1966 works are *Flour Arrangements*, a group of seven color photographs documenting varying arrangements of flour on Nauman's studio floor, and the famous *Self-Portrait as a Fountain.*

2. On Nauman's use of photography, see Los Angeles, p. 14.

3. For an interesting essay discussing the use of photography in printmaking, see Donna Stein, "Photography in Printmaking," *Print Review* 16 (1983), pp. 4–20; and more recently Boston, Museum of Fine Arts, *Photo-Image: Printmaking 60s to 90s,* exh. cat. by Clifford S. Ackley (1998).

4. Nauman, quoted in Los Angeles, pp. 66–68.

5. For the films—*Pinch Neck* (1968) and *Pulling Mouth* (1969)—see Cordes, nos. 119 and 152.

6. Infrared photography records the image of an object by using film sensitive to invisible infrared radiation, or heat, instead of to ordinary light. Although it was probably used in this instance because Nauman was recording himself in low light, an analogy can be made between the heat of the body being captured on film and the artist's larger interest in the malleable human form.

7. Minneapolis, Walker Art Center, *First Impressions: Early Prints by Forty-Six Contemporary Artists,* exh. cat. by Elizabeth Armstrong (1989), p. 68.

8. Paul Schimmel, "Pay Attention," in Minneapolis, p. 69.

Clown Torture, 1987, pp. 62–63

1. Nauman, quoted in Joan Simon, "Breaking the Silence: An Interview with Bruce Nauman," *Art in America* 76 (Sept. 1988), p. 203.

2. Other works by Nauman using the clown or jester figure as a central element include *Mean Clown Welcome* (1985; Cologne, private collection), *Clown Torture: Dark and Stormy Night with Laughter* (1987; Chicago, private collection), *Clown Torture: I'm Sorry and No, No, No, No* (1987; New York, private collection), *No, No New Museum* (1987; Stuttgart, Froehlich Collection), and *Double No* (1988; Stuttgart, Froelich Collection), among others.

3. Commenting on musicians and other performers, Nauman said: "It always seemed to me as if they were court jesters. They were responsible for providing something interesting for everybody else. . . . I always thought that was wrong and that everybody ought to be putting in a little more effort." Nauman, quoted in Kristine McKenna, "Bruce Nauman: Dan Weinberg Gallery," *Los Angeles Times,* Jan. 27, 1991, p. 4.

NOGUCHI, ISAMU

Altschuler, Bruce. *Isamu Noguchi.* New York, 1994.

Hunter, Sam. *Isamu Noguchi.* New York, [1978].

Minneapolis, Walker Art Center. *Noguchi's Imaginary Landscapes: An Exhibition.* Exh. cat. by Martin Friedman. 1978.

Noguchi, Isamu. *Isamu Noguchi: A Sculptor's World.* New York, [1968].

—. *Isamu Noguchi: Essays and Conversations.* Ed. by Diane Apostolos-Cappadona and Bruce Altschuler. New York, 1994.

Figure, 1946, pp. 14–15

1. Noguchi, quoted in New York, The Museum of Modern Art, *Fourteen Americans,* exh. cat. ed. by Dorothy C. Miller (1946), p. 39.

2. Noguchi [1968], p. 125.

POLKE, SIGMAR

Baden-Baden, Städtliche Kunsthalle Baden-Baden. *Sigmar Polke: Fotografien.* Exh. cat. 1990.
Bonn, Kunst- und Ausstellungshalle der Bundesrepublik Deutschland. *Sigmar Polke: Die drei Lügen der Malerei.* Exh. cat. 1997.
Cologne, Josef Haubrich Kunsthalle. *Sigmar Polke.* Exh. cat. 1984.
Los Angeles, Museum of Contemporary Art. *Sigmar Polke Photoworks: When Pictures Vanish.* Exh. cat. 1995.
Moos, David. "Sigmar Polke: Clairvoyant Memories." *art/text* 62 (Aug.–Oct. 1998), pp. 58–65.

Uri Geller Welcomes Unknown Beings from the Realm of Fables (Uri Geller empfängt fremde Wesen aus der Fabel), 1976, pp. 50–51

1. Polke, quoted in Tübingen, Kunsthalle Tübingen, *Sigmar Polke: Bilder, Tücher, Objekte, 1962–1971,* exh. cat. (1976), p. 127.

REINHARDT, AD

Bois, Yve Alain. "The Limit of Almost." In Los Angeles, Museum of Contemporary Art, et al. *Ad Reinhardt.* Exh. cat. 1991. Pp. 11–33.
Chicago, Museum of Contemporary Art. *Negotiating Rapture: The Power of Art to Transform Lives.* Exh. cat. ed. by Richard Francis. 1996. Pp. 42–43, 77–79.
Lippard, Lucy R. *Ad Reinhardt.* New York, 1981.
Reinhardt, Ad. *Art-as-Art: The Selected Writings of Ad Reinhardt.* Ed. and intro. by Barbara Rose. New York, 1975.
Vine, Naomi. "Mandala and Cross." *Art in America* 79 (Nov. 1991), pp. 124–33.

Abstract Painting 1960–1965, 1960–65, pp. 22–23

1. Ad Reinhardt, "Notes on the Black Paintings" (undated), in Reinhardt, p. 104.

RICHTER, GERHARD

Block, René, and Carl Vogel. *Grafik des Kapitalistischen Realismus.* Berlin, 1971.
Bonn, Kunst- und Ausstellungshalle der Bundesrepublik Deutschland. *Gerhard Richter.* 3 vols. Exh. cat. and cat. rais. 1993.
Bremen, Kunsthalle Bremen. *Gerhard Richter Editionen 1965–1993.* Exh. cat. 1993.
Butin, Hubertus. *Grafik des Kapitalistischen Realismus.* Frankfurt, 1992.
Chicago, Museum of Contemporary Art, et al. *Gerhard Richter, Paintings.* Exh. cat. by Roald Nasgaard, with essay by Michael Danoff; interview by Benjamin H. D. Buchloh. 1988.
Honisch, Dieter. *Gerhard Richter: Grafik 1965–1970.* Essen, 1970.
Krefeld, Museum Haus Lange Krefeld. *Gerhard Richter, Atlas der Fotos, Collagen und Skizzen.* Exh. cat. ed. by Helmut Friedel and Ulrich Wilmes. 1997.
Munich, Städtische Galerie im Lembachhaus. *Gerhard Richter Atlas.* Exh. cat. with essays by Armin Zweite. 1989.
Paoletti, John T. "Gerhard Richter: Ambiguity as an Agent of Awareness." *Print Collector's Newsletter* 19, 1 (Mar.–Apr. 1988), pp. 1–6.
Richter, Gerhard. *Gerhard Richter: The Daily Practice of Painting.* Ed. by Hans Ulrich Obrist; trans. by David Britt. London/Cambridge, Mass., 1995.
Rotterdam, Museum Boymans-van Beuningen. *Gerhard Richter 1988/89.* Exh. cat. 1989.
Shapiro, Michael Edward. *Gerhard Richter Paintings, Prints, and Photographs in the Collection of the Saint Louis Art Museum.* St. Louis, 1992.

Mouth (Mund), 1963, pp. 24–25

1. Richter made his early Photo Paintings by squaring up photographic images and reproducing them freehand. Later, he painted from photographs projected onto the canvas.

2. Richter confirmed that *Mouth*'s subject is Bardot in an unpublished interview with Tim Peterson of Lannan Foundation, Los Angeles (Feb. 8, 1993).

3. Richter, quoted in ibid.

Woman Descending the Staircase (Frau die Treppe herabgehend), 1965, pp. 28–29

1. Munich, p. 29.

2. "Interview with Jonas Storsve, 1991," in Richter, pp. 225–26. *Ema* was the first painting Richter produced from a photograph that he had taken himself, rather than found.

3. Ibid.

Mrs. Wolleh with Children (Frau Wolleh mit Kindern), 1968, pp. 34–35

1. This account of the painting's origin was confirmed on behalf of Gerhard Richter by his assistant Lydia Wirtz, in an undated letter to Lisa Lyons of Lannan Foundation, Los Angeles.

9 Objects (9 Objekte), 1968, pp. 36–37

1. Shapiro, p. 48. Richter's extensive use of photo-offset lithography, as opposed to traditional, autographic, hand lithography, underscores his originality in this area. Previously, artists were expected to mark the matrix with their own hand, and/or proofs were taken directly by hand. Richter let the machine do the work for him.

2. Paoletti, p. 2.

3. Ibid., p. 3.

4. According to Paoletti (ibid., p. 5), Richter was interested in Conceptual Art, especially the work of LeWitt, with which he felt some sympathy. Here, Richter subtly mocked the solemn and rigorous attitude that LeWitt has brought to his use of the cube motif, and, at the same time, seemed to revel in LeWitt's idea that "illogical judgments lead to new experience" (sentence 4 in LeWitt's "Sentences on Conceptual Art," in Grégoire Müller, *The New Avant-Garde: Issues for the Art of the Seventies* [New York, 1972], p. 46).

Flowers (Blumen), 1993, pp. 82–83

1. Munich, pp. 143–45.

2. "Interview with Hans Ulrich Obrist, 1993," in Richter, p. 268.

3. Ibid.

4. Ibid., pp. 268–69.

RUFF, THOMAS

Amsterdam, Stedelijk Museum, et al. *Thomas Ruff: Portretten, Huizen, Sterren.* Exh. cat. 1990.

Brauchitsch, Boris von. *Thomas Ruff*. Frankfurt am Main, 1992.
Frankfurt am Main, Museum Schloss Hardenberg, et al. *Thomas Ruff: Porträts*. Exh. cat. 1988.
Ruff, Thomas. *Thomas Ruff: Andere Porträts + 3D*. Ostfildern, 1995.

Untitled (Ralph Müller), 1986; *Untitled*, 1988; *Untitled*, 1988, pp. 54–57

1. Ruff, quoted in an interview by Stephan Dillemuth, "That remains to be seen. Many things are conceivable that have little basis in reality," in Ruff, p. 18.

2. Ruff, quoted in Brauchitsch, p. 24.

3. Ibid., pp. 23–24.

4. Ruff, p. 18.

5. Dillemuth observed of the star studies, "These large-format photographs (260 x 188 cm) rob star-gazing of its romanticism." Ibid., p. 26.

6. Ibid., p. 18.

7. Ruff, quoted in Brauchitsch, p. 24.

8. Ruff, p. 18. Undeniably, Ruff is someone who recycles imagery by others. These models for his work range from the massive documentation of the German people by the early twentieth-century photographer August Sander to the immense portraits of art-school friends by the late twentieth-century American painter Chuck Close (see pp. 74–75).

RUPPERSBERG, ALLEN

Los Angeles, Museum of Contemporary Art. *Allen Ruppersberg: The Secret of Life and Death*. Exh. cat. by Howard Singerman. 1985.
Plagens, Peter. "Ruppersberg's Encyclopedia." *Art in America* 73 (Dec. 1985), pp. 84–93.
Weelden, Dirk van. *Allen Ruppersberg: A Different Kind of Never-Never-Land*. Amsterdam, 1992.

Remainders: Novel, Sculpture, Film, 1991, pp. 78–79

1. *Remainders: Novel, Sculpture, Film* was included in an exhibition entitled "Tables: Selections from the Lannan Foundation Collection" at Lannan Foundation, Los Angeles, where visitors were permitted to handle and read the individual books. An exhibition context that allows for the work to function as an interactive sculpture invites a somewhat different reading than the one offered here.

2. The dichotomy between seeing and reading, or between looking and knowing, is at the heart of an earlier series of work by Ruppersberg. *Seeing and Believing* (1972) is a two-part photographic piece: *Seeing* consists of six black-and-white exterior shots of six older California bungalows; *Believing* consists of six shots of domestic interiors. The juxtaposition of both parts makes it obvious that the interior shots, with their modern design and architecture, do not correspond to the houses represented in the exterior shots.

RUSCHA, EDWARD

Auckland, Auckland City Art Gallery. *Graphic Works by Edward Ruscha*. Exh. cat. by Andrew Bogel. 1978.
Lake Worth, Fla., Lannan Museum. *Edward Ruscha: Words Without Thoughts Never to Heaven Go*. Exh. cat. 1988.

New York, Gagosian Gallery. *Edward Ruscha, Romance with Liquids: Paintings 1966–1969*. Exh. cat. by Yve Alain Bois. 1993.

F House, 1987, pp. 60–61

1. Robert Landau, "A Conversation with Edward Ruscha," in *Outrageous L.A.* (San Francisco, 1984), p. 9.

2. Lake Worth, Fla., p. 31.

SAMARAS, LUCAS

Glimcher, Arnold B. "Lucas Samaras: Photo-Transformations." In Long Beach, Calif., California State University, Art Galleries. *Photo-Transformations*. Exh. cat. ed. by Constance W. Glenn. 1975.
Lifson, Ben. "Photo-Transformations." In *Samaras: The Photographs of Lucas Samaras*. New York, 1989. Pp. 42–45.
New York, Pace Gallery. *Lucas Samaras, Pastels*. Exh. cat. by Milly Glimcher. 1993.
Schjeldahl, Peter. "Lucas Samaras: The Pastels." In Denver, Denver Art Museum. *Samaras Pastels*. Exh. cat. by Dianne Perry Vanderlip. 1981. Pp. 6–16.

Phototransformation (10/25/73), 1973; *Phototransformation (4/4/76)*, 1976; *Phototransformation (7/31/76)*, 1976, pp. 48–49

1. It is important to note that the Polaroid technology available to Samaras twenty-five years ago was substantially different from that in use today. Contemporary Polaroid film can no longer be manipulated in exactly the same way, due to advances in both the photograph casing and the developing process.

SMITH, KIKI

Amsterdam, Institute of Contemporary Art. *Kiki Smith*. Exh. cat. 1990.
Columbus, Oh., Ohio State University, Wexner Center for the Arts, et al. *Kiki Smith*. Exh. cat. by Linda Shearer. 1992.
London, Whitechapel Art Gallery. *Kiki Smith*. Exh. cat. by Jo Anna Isaak. 1995.
Montreal, Montreal Museum of Fine Arts, et al. *Kiki Smith*. Exh. cat. by Pierre Théberge. 1996.
Posner, Helaine. *Kiki Smith*. Boston, 1998.

Untitled, 1988, pp. 64–65

1. London, p. 22.

2. Michael Boodro, "Blood, Spit, and Beauty," *ARTnews* 93 (Mar. 1994), p. 129.

3. Smith most frequently features the specifically female body in her work, in many cases selecting historical women from Christianity, Judaism, and various Eastern religions as her primary subjects.

4. London, p. 31.

STILL, CLYFFORD

Basel, Kunsthalle Basel, et al. *Clyfford Still, 1904–1980: The Buffalo and San Francisco Collections*. Exh. cat. by Thomas Kellerin. 1992.
New York, The Metropolitan Museum of Art. *Clyfford Still*. Exh. cat. 1979.

Photography Credits

Unless otherwise noted, all works in the Art Institute's collections were photographed by the Department of Imaging, Alan Newman, Executive Director. Permission to reproduce the works of art in this volume has been provided by the artists or their representatives. The following credits apply to all images for which separate acknowledgment is due. They are arranged alphabetically by artist and are keyed to page numbers. Multiple works by individual artists are distinguished by numbers from the Checklist of the Lannan Collection (pp. 86–97).

Ahearn, John, courtesy Brooke Alexander, New York, pp. 53, 86 [photo: Susan Einstein]. Andre, Carl, © Carl Andre/Licensed by VAGA, New York, N.Y., p. 86 [photo: courtesy AIC]. Artschwager, Richard, © 1999 Richard Artschwager/Artists Rights Society (ARS), New York, pp. 27, 86 [photo: Susan Einstein]. Burton, Scott, Scott Burton Estate, courtesy Max Protetch Gallery, New York, no. 5, pp. 47, 86 [photo: courtesy AIC]; no. 6, p. 86 [photo: courtesy AIC]; no. 7, p. 86 [photo: Susan Einstein]; fig. 1, p. 46 [photo from Düsseldorf, Kunstverein für die Rheinlande und Westfalen, *Scott Burton: Skulpturen 1980–89*, exh. cat. by Jiri Svestka (1989), p. 7 (fig. 6)]. Celmins, Vija, courtesy McKee Gallery, New York, no. 8, pp. 31, 86 [photo: Susan Einstein]; no. 9, p. 86 [photo: courtesy AIC]. Close, Chuck, courtesy PaceWildenstein, New York, no. 10, p. 87 [photo: courtesy AIC]; no. 11, p. 87 [photo: Susan Einstein]; no. 12, p. 87 [photo: Susan Einstein]; no. 13, pp. 3 (detail), 75, 87 [photo: courtesy AIC]; no. 14, p. 87 [photo: Susan Einstein]; no. 15, pp. 77, 88 [photo: Susan Einstein]; no. 16, p. 89 [photo: courtesy AIC]; fig. 1, p. 76 [Lannan Foundation]. DeFeo, Jay, © 1999 The Estate of Jay DeFeo/Artists Rights Society (ARS), New York, pp. 19, 89 [photo: Susan Einstein]. Francis, Sam, © 1999 The Estate of Sam Francis/Artists Rights Society (ARS), New York, pp. 17, 89 [photo: courtesy AIC]. Friedman, Tom, courtesy Feature, Inc., New York, pp. 81, 89 [photo: Susan Einstein]. Gonzalez-Torres, Felix, courtesy The Estate of Felix Gonzalez-Torres/Andrea Rosen Gallery Inc., New York, pp. 85, 90 [photo: Peter Muscato]. Hammons, David, courtesy A. C. Hudgins, pp. 43, 90 [photo: Susan Einstein]. Hill, Gary, courtesy Donald Young Gallery, pp. 73, 90 [photo: courtesy AIC]. Jaar, Alfredo, courtesy Alfredo Jaar Studio, pp. 59, 91 [photo: courtesy AIC]. Jensen, Alfred, © 1999 The Estate of Alfred Jensen/Artists Rights Society (ARS), New York, p. 33, 91 [photo: courtesy AIC]. Kelley, Mike, courtesy Metro Pictures, New York, pp. 67, 91 [photo: Douglas M. Parker Studio]. Marden, Brice, © 1999 Brice Marden/Artists Rights Society (ARS), New York, no. 38, pp. 45, 91 [photo: Tom Vinetz]; no. 39, pp. 91–92 [photos courtesy AIC]. Matisse, Henri, © 1999 Succession H. Matisse, Paris/Artists Rights Society (ARS), New York, fig. 1, p. 12 [photo: courtesy AIC]. Morris, Robert, © Robert Morris/Artists Rights Society (ARS), New York, p. 92 [photo: Susan Einstein]. Motherwell, Robert, © Dedalus Foundation/Licensed by VAGA, New York, NY, pp. 13, 92 [photo: courtesy AIC]. Nauman, Bruce, © 1999 Bruce Nauman/Artists Rights Society (ARS), New York, no. 43, pp. 39, 92 [photo: Susan Einstein]; no. 44, pp. 41, 92–93 [photos: Susan Einstein]; no. 45, p. 93 [photo: courtesy AIC]; no. 46, pp. 63, 93 [photos: courtesy AIC]. Noguchi, Isamu, courtesy The Isamu Noguchi Foundation, pp. 15, 93 [photos: courtesy AIC]; fig. 1, p. 14 [photo from *The Art Institute of Chicago Bulletin* 41, 7 (Dec. 1947), p. 89]. Polke, Sigmar, courtesy Michael Werner Gallery, New York, pp. 3 (detail), 51, 93 [photos: Susan Einstein]. Reinhardt, Ad, © 1999 The Estate of Ad Reinhardt/Artists Rights Society (ARS), New York, pp. 23, 93 [photo: Susan Einstein]. Richter, Gerhard, courtesy Marion Goodman Gallery, New York, no. 50, pp. 25, 93 [photo: courtesy AIC]; no. 51, pp. 3 (detail), 29, 94 [photo: courtesy AIC]; no. 52, pp. 35, 94 [photo: Susan Einstein]; no. 53, pp. 37, 94 [photo: Susan Einstein]; no. 54, p. 94 [photo: courtesy AIC]; no. 55, p. 94 [photo: courtesy AIC]; no. 56, pp. 69–71, 94 [photos: Susan Einstein]; no. 57, p. 95 [photo: courtesy AIC]; no. 58, p. 95 [photo: courtesy AIC]; no. 59, p. 95 [photo: courtesy AIC]; no. 60, pp. 83, 95 [photo: Susan Einstein]; fig. 1, p. 28 [photo from Munich, Städtische Galerie im Lembachhaus, *Gerhard Richter Atlas*, exh. cat. with essays by Armin Zweite (1989), p. 13]. Ruff, Thomas, © 1999 Artists Rights Society (ARS), New York/VG Bild-Kunst, Bonn, pp. 55–57, 95 [photos: Susan Einstein]. Ruppersberg, Allen, courtesy Gorney Bravin + Lee, New York, pp. 79, 95 [photo: Susan Einstein]. Ruscha, Edward, courtesy Leo Castelli, New York, no. 65, p. 96 [photo: Susan Einstein]; no. 66, pp. 61, 96 [photo: courtesy AIC]. Samaras, Lucas, courtesy PaceWildenstein, New York, no. 67, pp. 48, 96 [photo: courtesy AIC]; no. 68, p. 96 [photo: courtesy AIC]; no. 69, pp. 49, 96 [photo: Susan Einstein]; no. 70, pp. 49, 96 [photo: Susan Einstein]; no. 71, pp. 49, 96 [photo: Susan Einstein]. Smith, Kiki, courtesy PaceWildenstein, New York, pp. 65, 97 [photo: Susan Einstein]. Smithson, Robert, © The Estate of Robert Smithson/Licensed by VAGA, New York, N.Y., p. 97 [photo: courtesy AIC]. Still, Clyfford, courtesy Mrs. Clyfford Still, pp. 21, 97 [photo: courtesy AIC]. All additional checklist photography courtesy The Art Institute of Chicago. Strick essay: fig. 1, p. 7 [photo: courtesy Lannan Foundation]; fig. 2, p. 9 [photo: courtesy AIC].